SUNRISE AT CAMPOBELLO

A Play in Three Acts

BY DORE SCHARY

★

★

DRAMATISTS
PLAY SERVICE
INC.

For My Best Friend
MIRIAM

I take this opportunity to acknowledge the invaluable aid received from personal recollections and comments by Mrs. Eleanor Roosevelt, Mrs. James Halsted, Congressman James Roosevelt and Mr. Franklin D. Roosevelt, Jr.

I also extend deep appreciation to the authors of the vast bibliography concerning the life, times and works of Franklin D. Roosevelt.

Finally, my sincere thanks to Dr. Herman Kahn, director of the Hyde Park Memorial Library, and to his assistant, Raymond Corry, and to the entire staff of the Library for their constant guidance and aid.

DORE SCHARY

SUNRISE AT CAMPOBELLO was first presented by The Theatre Guild and Dore Schary at the Cort Theatre, New York City, on January 30, 1958. It was directed by Vincent J. Donehue, and the production was designed and lighted by Ralph Alswang. The cast was as follows:

(IN ORDER OF APPEARANCE)

ANNA ROOSEVELT	*Roni Dengel*
ELEANOR ROOSEVELT	*Mary Fickett*
FRANKLIN D. ROOSEVELT, JR.	*Kenneth Kakos*
JAMES ROOSEVELT	*James Bonnet*
ELLIOTT ROOSEVELT	*Perry Skaar*
EDWARD	*James Earl Jones*
FRANKLIN DELANO ROOSEVELT	*Ralph Bellamy*
JOHN ROOSEVELT	*Jeffrey Rowland*
MARIE	*Ethel Everett*
LOUIS MCHENRY HOWE	*Henry Jones*
MRS. SARA DELANO ROOSEVELT	*Anne Seymour*
MISS MARGUERITE (MISSY) LEHAND	*Mary Welch*
DOCTOR BENNET	*James Reese*
FRANKLIN CALDER	*William Fort*
STRETCHER BEARERS	*Edwin Phillips, Vincent Dowling, Floyd Curtis*
MR. BRIMMER	*Clifford Carpenter*
MR. LASSITER	*Richard Robbins*
GOVERNOR ALFRED E. SMITH	*Alan Bunce*
DALY	*Jerry Crews*
POLICEMAN	*Floyd Curtis*
SENATOR WALSH	*Vincent Dowling*
A SPEAKER	*Edwin Phillips*

SYNOPSIS OF SCENES

ACT ONE

Scene 1—Campobello, August 10, 1921
Scene 2—The Same, September 1, 1921
Scene 3—The Same, September 13, 1921

ACT TWO

Scene 1—New York, May 1922
Scene 2—The Same, January 1923

ACT THREE

Scene 1—New York, May 1924
Scene 2—Madison Square Garden (an anteroom)
       June 26, 1924
Scene 3—The Platform, a few moments later

NOTE

Throughout the play the word "mama" is pronounced "ma*ma*" with the accent always on the second syllable.

NOTE

PROPERTY PLOT

Act I, Scene 1

Preset

Furniture

Ottoman D.R.
Table D.C.
2 chairs—armed R. and L. of
Table D.C.
Table U.C.
Porcelain umbrella stand L. of
Table U.C.
Waste basket R. of Table U.C.
Chair U.L. toward kitchen
Table U.L.
Mantel L.
Chaise Longue D.L.

Decorative Props

Curtains, window U.L.
Clock on wall U.C.
Picture below clock
Megaphone above umbrella stand
Pennants strung across window U.L.
Harvard Pennant below Megaphone
Pictures on staircase wall
Photograph album on Window Seat
Vase on second shelf of mantel
4 ornate pieces on mantel
Ornate piece table U.C.

Hand Props on Stage

4 croquet mallets (2 upright, 2
down) R. window seat
Sailboat on R. window sill
Tennis racquet in L. window
sill U.R.C.
Jigsaw puzzle Table D.C. (L. side)

Student lamp Table U.C.
Ashtray table U.C.
Tennis racquet, umbrella, 2 pieces
of clothing—in Umbrella stand
Vase of flowers Table U.L.
Double Ashtray R. side of Table U.L.
Newspaper—Table U.L.
Letter from B.S.A. Table U.L.
Letter from Mama—Table U.L.
Lamp—Table U.L.
Scotch Bottle and glass—Closet
under stairs
Bag of golf clubs L. of Closet door
2 Pillows on Chaise
Sewing Basket with chartreuse wool
and a variety of colors with needles
bottom shelf of table D.C.
Ashtray Table D.C. (Double)
2 Pillows in chair R. of Table D.C.
(Green and yellow)
Window U.R. open
Door U.L.C. open with spring on
screen

Prop Table off R. (11)

1 small picnic basket—Anna
1 Sweater—Anna
1 Bathing cap—Anna
1 Towel—Anna
1 Towel—James
1 Towel—Elliott
1 Towel—Franklin Jr.
1 Towel—Johnnie
1 Sweater—James
1 Sweater—Elliott

1 Sweater—FRANKLIN JR.
1 Sweater—JOHNNY
2 Canoe paddles—JAMES
Pennant and rope—JAMES

Prop Table off L. *(11)*

1 small copy of "Julius Caesar"
1 Large Volume of Shakespearean
  plays

List of Groceries and pencil
  —EDWARD
Baseball and Mitt—FRANKLIN JR.
Hair Ribbon—ANNA
Baseball mitt—ELEANOR
2 Sweaters (blue and chartreuse)
  —ELEANOR
Piece of wood and scout knife
  —ELLIOTT

ACT ONE

Scene 1

It is August tenth, 1921. We are in the large living room of Franklin Delano Roosevelt's summer home at Campobello, New Brunswick, Canada. It is a homey, sprawling summer lodge. Picture windows reveal the firs and pines of the forest and allow us to view part of the bay. The sky is pink with the coming dusk. A porch runs along the outside of the house and we can see some of it. The atmosphere is woodsy and comfortable, not elegant or fancy, but rather a house that has seen hard wear by an energetic and healthy family. There are no electric lights. At night the house is illuminated by kerosene lamps, many of which are placed about the room.

The door to the kitchen and dining room is D.R. A large bay window with a window seat runs from the D.R. door, slanting up to R.C., in the back wall. The porch is seen beyond this window. A rattan table stands in front of the window seat. An arched window is in the rear wall L. of the bay window. Before it is another table, and just to the L. of this table, a waste basket. An umbrella stand, which also serves as a clothes rack, is L. of the arched window and just R. of the screen door U.L.C. which leads out to the porch. There is another window L. of the screen door, through which we also see the porch. A flight of steps, two leading up to a landing, and then more steps going upstairs is at L. In the rear, between the stairs and the L. window is a passageway to a side room. Under the stairs, D.L. is a table. D.S. of the table, a closet in which liquor is kept. The fireplace is D.L., below the closet. In the center of the room are a round rattan table and two rattan chairs L. and R. of it. A chaise longue (also referred to as the couch) is L.C., and ottoman D.R. A megaphone hangs on the rear wall above the umbrella stand. There are lamps on most of the tables.

The stage is bare. Then Anna, wearing a bathing suit and carrying a picnic basket, can be glimpsed coming across the porch from R. to L. She enters screen door U.L.C.

11

ANNA. (*As she crosses into the house, crosses to stairs.*) Mother! (*Then louder.*) Mother! (*Eleanor appears on the steps leading down into the room. She is dressed in a white flannel skirt and blue sweater and she wears white sneakers.*)

ELEANOR. Yes, Anna? (*Crosses D.C.*)

ANNA. Mother, you missed all the fun. (*Puts basket on stairs.*) After sailing, we went swimming in the lagoon and then we trotted across the spit and dove into the bay.

ELEANOR. It sounds very strenuous. I'm delighted I never learned how to swim. (*She motions Anna upstairs. Anna smiles and starts up the steps.*) If you're through with the picnic I'd better take the basket. (*Anna crosses C., smiles, exits on stairs, hands Eleanor the basket and continues up the stairs. Franklin Jr., wearing a bathing suit storms across porch from R. to L. and into house from screen door. He throws his towel and his sweater down near the clothes rack.*)

FRANKLIN JR. (*Wearily.*) Hello, mother. (*Crosses D.L., flops on couch.*)

ELEANOR. Hello, Franklin. (*He crosses to the couch and collapses.*) Franklin, I know you're on the verge of exhaustion, but you are to get up from the couch and put your towel and sweater where they belong. (*Crosses to window seat—puts picnic basket down.*)

FRANKLIN JR. Now?

ELEANOR. (*Crosses U.R.*) Now. (*Franklin Jr. groans his way from the couch, picks up the sweater and towel, puts them on the rack [umbrella stand], and then staggers back to the couch. Eleanor exits to the kitchen D.R. Jimmy and Elliott now enter from the porch through screen door. Both of them are also wearing bathing suits. They too toss their towels and sweaters more or less in the direction of the clothes rack.*)

JIMMY. You paddle your way along like a polliwog. Your hands have to hit the water clean. That's the only way to get pull into your strokes—like this.

ELLIOTT. (*Throws towel on window seat.*) You aren't exactly champion of the world, you know.

JIMMY. I'm only telling you what Pa told me. He told it to all of us but you don't listen. Elliott, you never listen. (*Elliott throws other towel on floor.*) (*By now Elliott has become aware of Franklin Jr. stretched out on the couch and he silently indicates to Jimmy that they do something about this. Jimmy and Elliott begin to tiptoe toward the couch. Franklin Jr., though his back is to both of them, senses that he is about to be attacked.*)

FRANKLIN JR. You leave me alone. (*Elliott and Jimmy push him off the couch, which Jimmy immediately appropriates. Elliott wrestles Franklin.*) THAT WAS A ROTTEN THING TO DO. That was a real rotten thing to do. (*Eleanor appears from the kitchen D.R.*)

ELEANOR. (*Crosses C.*) Good evening, Jimmy, Elliott.

JIMMY. Mother, you missed the real fun. We finished up swimming—

ELEANOR. Anna told me all about it.

ELLIOTT. It was freezing—absolutely freezing.

ELEANOR. Now, up. UP! (*The boys begin picking up their suits and towels.*) Where's Johnny?

JIMMY. He's with Father on the dock. (*Eleanor crosses over to a cardboard megaphone that hangs near the door U.L.C. Jimmy calls out with mock alarm.*) Oh, no, Mother!

ELEANOR. It's time they were home. (*Crosses U.R. to window seat.*) (*She calls out.*) Franklin! Johnny! (*Elliott and Franklin Jr. cross U.L.*) (*Then even louder.*) Franklin! Johnny! (*Franklin Jr. and Elliott cross to window seat.*)

JIMMY. Mother, I hate to say this but your voice coming through there sounds like the call to judgment.

ELEANOR. That's enough from you, Mr. James Roosevelt. Upstairs. All of you—upstairs. (*She points to the upper floor. The boys nod and then form a group. They hide their right fists behind their backs and then extend their hands with fingers outstretched. Jimmy and Elliott appear disgusted.*)

FRANKLIN JR. ONE! TWO! THREE! This time I win. (*Jimmy and Elliott make a seat for Franklin Jr. with their hands and carry him up the steps groaning loudly at his weight.*)

ELLIOTT. He's stuffed with lead—all lead. (*Eleanor calls through the megaphone.*)

ELEANOR. Franklin! Johnny! (*She hangs up the megaphone as Edward enters from kitchen D.R. with a slip of paper and a pencil.*)

13

EDWARD. (U.R.) Mrs. McGowan says she needs all this from town, Mrs. Roosevelt. (*Eleanor studies the list.*)

ELEANOR. (*Crosses* C. *with Edward at* C. *table.*) We'll pick everything tomorrow, Edward. (*She returns the list to Edward.*) And please, add hard candy and chocolate. Also some cigarettes for Mr. Roosevelt. (*Edward makes a note. Anna, now dressed in casual clothes comes down the steps. She carries a book.*)

ANNA. (*As she enters from upstairs.*) Mother, I don't see why you picked Julius Caesar for us to read tonight. All the good parts are for men.

ELEANOR. You and I, like all the others, will double up in parts.

ANNA. (*On landing.*) I'd like to read Brutus.

ELEANOR. Your father makes the final decisions on casting. Please tell Mrs. McGowan that we're going sailing and picnicking tomorrow again. I'll talk with her later about the lunch.

EDWARD. Yes ma'am.

ANNA (*Crosses* D.R.) Mother, we'd all appreciate it if we could get something other than fried chicken and hardboiled eggs.

ELEANOR. I thought tomorrow we'd try fried eggs and hard-boiled chicken. (*Anna sits* D.R. *on ottoman.*)

FDR. (*Calling as he crosses the porch from* R. *to* L. *He wears a white cap, a bathing suit and a robe.*) Eleanor, they heard you clean across to Eastport.

ELEANOR. Stand by, the Captain is home.

FDR. Come on slowpoke. (*He enters through screen door* U.L.C.) Hello, Eleanor, Sis. (*Crosses to bay window.*) Hello, small fry. (*He lifts Johnny through the bay window and into the room.*)

ANNA. Last again. The runt.

JOHNNY. Don't call me runt. I'm Johnny.

FDR. (*Crosses* D.L.) You tell her, sonny. Eleanor, you missed all the fun—

ELEANOR. (*Crosses to Johnny with towel.*) So Anna, James, Elliott and Franklin Jr. have told me. (*Marie enters from upstairs.*)

MARIE. (*Crosses to Johnny and kneels.*) Oh, there you are, my friend Johnnie.

JOHNNY. (*Crosses to FDR.*) Marie, I don't want to go upstairs.

ELEANOR. (*Crosses* C.) Yes you do.

14

JOHNNY. (*Crosses to FDR.*) Father?

MARIE. Johnnie, *il faut t'habiller pour diner.*

JOHNNY. *Un moment, s'il vous plait. Papa—comment va tu?*

FDR. *Ca va bien.* I'll make your journey upstairs a pleasant one. (*FDR. sweeps Johnny up on his back and races up the steps with him. Johnny squeals with delight. Marie starts up after them.*)

JOHNNY. GIDYAP! GIDYAP!

MARIE. *Voila,* Johnnie! Dinner as usual, Mrs. Roosevelt? (*Exits upstairs.*)

ELEANOR. Yes, Marie, six-thirty. (*We hear the voices of the boys as they greet their father's arrival upstairs.*)

JIMMY. (*Offstage.*) Hello, father. Why don't you do that for me?

ELLIOTT. (*Offstage.*) I don't think I like Shakespeare at all.

ANNA. Boys are so loud and noisy. Mother, how you put up with the four of them I don't know.

ELEANOR. The four boys are easy, Anna. It's the one girl.

ANNA. (*Rather proud.*) Do you think I'm difficult?

ELEANOR. I think you feel surrounded by the men in the family.

ANNA. (*Crosses C.*) (*Not at all perturbed.*) Before Granny went to Europe she told me she thinks you're too severe with me.

ELEANOR. I'm aware of your chats with Granny.

ANNA. (*Confidentially.*) Actually, Granny spoils us. The boys can talk her out of anything. All they have to do is speak a little French or agree with her.

ELEANOR. What about you?

ANNA. Oh, of course, so can I. (*FDR has just been coming down the steps and as he speaks he picks up a letter and a newspaper.*)

FDR. So can you what?

ANNA. What?

FDR. (*Crosses to couch D.L. Gets paper and letter.*) I heard you say so can I. (*Puts letter in pocket.*)

ANNA. (*Crosses D.R., sits on ottoman.*) Oh— Talk Granny out of anything I want, just like the boys. Especially if I agree with her when she says something about Mr. Howe. (*Jimmy comes downstairs dressed. He carries a copy of Julius Caesar.*)

JIMMY. (*On landing.*) Father, is Mr. Howe coming back here?

FDR. No, he's tied up in Washington.

ELEANOR. Jimmy, why do you ask?

15

JIMMY. (*Crosses* U.L.) Nothing.

FDR. (*Crosses* U.L.) Why do you ask—nothing? What kind of English is that? (*Slowly, looking at Jimmy.*) Why do you ask?

JIMMY. For no reason.

FDR. (*Crosses to Anna* D.R.) That's better.

ELEANOR. But you had a reason, Jimmy. I want you to tell me.

JIMMY. (*Sits* D.L. *on couch.*) Well, usually he rooms next to me and that coughing and wheezing he does so much keeps me up at night. And if he burns that incense to stop the coughing, that's worse than anything.

FDR. You never appear to be suffering from a lack of sleep.

JIMMY. Father, I'm serious.

FDR. Jimmy, I'm serious too. I want no criticism of or complaints about Mr. Louis Howe from you or anyone else. Is that understood?

JIMMY. (*Rises.*) Understood.

ANNA. Granny always says that Mr. Howe—

FDR. I know all about Granny's opinions of Mr. Howe and I don't want them repeated by you. Now I would appreciate it if you and Jimmy would do some rehearsing for tonight's reading. (*The cross and exit through door* D.R.) Babs, how about a hard drink? I feel tired and a little achy. That's the first swim I've had in years that didn't refresh me. (*Crosses* C. *to Eleanor.*)

ELEANOR. You should be more careful.

FDR. Eleanor, I am not catching another cold, and I am not becoming an alcoholic. (*Puts cigarette in holder.*)

ELEANOR. (*Crosses* D.L. *to closet, prepares drink.*) I just want you to get out of that wet suit.

FDR. In a few minutes. It's a pleasure to open a paper and see my name out of it. (*Crosses* D.L.) This is a tidy item. Almost six million unemployed, and Harding playing his tuba. (*Throws cap on* D.L.C. *chair.*) Thanks, Babs. Good. That'll take the chill out of my bones. (*Sits* D.L. *Eleanor crosses* R. *of couch.*) I often think of something Woodrow Wilson said to me: "It is only once in a generation that a people can be lifted above material things. That is why conservative government is in the saddle for two thirds of the time."

16

ELEANOR. (*Crosses* C., *takes sweater.*) Louie insists that you can reverse the trend.

FDR. Yes, after having wet nursed my public relations for ten years. He doesn't like my staying in this Wall Street job. Says it's hardly the place for a dedicated progressive. (*Eleanor sits* D.L.)

ELEANOR. Well, Franklin, is it?

FDR. Babs, it's five hundred a week. And confidentially, Mrs. R., the light on my political horizon appears rather dim and dark. There is nothing so unattractive to a party as a defeated candidate.

ELEANOR. I hardly think you, as the Vice-Presidential candidate, will be held responsible for the defeat of the Democratic party. After all, Cox ran for the Presidency, not you. (*Rises, crosses* U.L., *gives FDR ashtray.*)

FDR. (*Eleanor crosses* D.L., *sits.*) Babs, I've weathered battles with Tammany Hall, seven years in the Navy Department, and Mama's massive objections to policies, which she considers one step higher than garbage collecting. I am quite sure that Wall Street will not corrupt my political convictions.

ELEANOR. That's a comfort.

FDR. And if I get into deep water, keep your eye on me, Babs.

ELEANOR. God takes man into deep water not to drown him but to cleanse him.

FDR. Helpful hint from helpful wife. Thank you, ma'am, thank you kindly. (*Elliott and Franklin Jr. enter* D.R.)

ELLIOTT. Ma, we're hungry. (*FDR rises, crosses to* D.R.C. *chair.*)

ELEANOR. It'll only be a few minutes now.

FDR. (*Crosses* C.) Ah, from mama. From Granny!

FRANKLIN JR. What does Granny say? (*Anna and Jimmy enter* D.R.)

ANNA. (*Crosses* C.) Father, we have to decide who's going to read what. (*James sits* D.R.) (*Johnny comes downstairs, followed by Marie.*)

FDR. (*Sits* R. *of* C. *table.*) (*Anna is* R.—*Franklin Jr.* C., *Elliott* L.) As you know, we will all have to read a variety of parts. But the main assignments are as follows: your mother will read Calpurnia. Anna, you shall read Portia, and Cinna the poet and Octavius. You, Jimmy, shall read Brutus.

JIMMY. I've been studying Antony.

17

FDR. I shall read Marc Antony. You are Brutus. And you, Elliott, will make a fine Cassius. You, Franklin, have the round look of Casca. And you, Johnny, shall be the mobs, the citizens, (*Johnny and Marie enter*) and the sounds of battle. (*Johnny crosses* C. *with Marie.*) And you, Marie, shall be Julius Caesar.

MARIE. *Merci!*

FDR. Probably one of my greatest strokes of casting. (*Anna takes book, crosses to window seat.*)

FRANKLIN JR. What's in Granny's letter?

ANNA. (*Crosses* U.R., *sits.*) Please tell us, father.

FDR. Well, let's see. Granny has moved to London to visit Cousin Muriel, whose slight operation was apparently successful. Though mama doesn't have a high opinion of British medicine. Granny doesn't approve of Muriel's bed. Too hard.

JIMMY. She says my bed's too soft.

FDR. Granny believes in hard beds for men and soft beds for women.

ELEANOR. Hear!

FDR. Now, Granny may sail on the twenty-fourth, which would bring her home on the thirty-first—or a week later, which would bring her home September the seventh. She may stay. She loves the hotel. "Much love to the precious children. I expect to find a French family on my return. Devotedly, Mama." That means Mama expects you all to be speaking perfect French. *Ici on parle Francais!* (*Edward enters* D.R., *crosses* U.L.)

EDWARD. (U.L.) Mrs. Roosevelt, dinner's ready.

ELEANOR. Thank you, Edward.

ELLIOTT. (*Crosses* U.L.) What has Mrs. McGowan got to eat tonight?

ELEANOR. Whatever Mrs. McGowan has to eat you will enjoy.

ELLIOTT. I'm sure of that, mother. I just wanted to know.

ELEANOR. Let life surprise you, Elliott. It's more fun that way. (*She directs the children into the dining room* D.R.)

JIMMY. (*Crosses* C.) (*Sitting next to FDR.*) How's the arm, father? (*Everybody* C.)

ELEANOR. Franklin!

FDR. This will only take a moment, Babs. (*He puts his arm on the table opposite Jimmy. They clasp hands. The children group*

18

around. Jimmy is already straining every muscle.) Ready? (*Warn Slow* CURTAIN.)

JIMMY. Ready. (*FDR puts Jimmy's arm down, rolling him to the floor.*)

FDR. Undefeated and still champion. (*The kids move out towards the dining room* D.R. *FDR saunters over to the bay window.*) This time of day is always the best. (*Crosses* U.R.) It's as if the sun (*Eleanor crosses* U.L.) were standing still for a last glimpse, a long lingering look before saying goodnight.

ELEANOR. It's a nice quiet time.

FDR. I wish I could stay until after Labor Day. (*Suddenly he stumbles and grabs his back. He recovers. Eleanor goes to him at* U.R.)

ELEANOR. Franklin?

FDR. Must be a spot of lumbago. (*Eleanor puts her hand to his brow.*) I don't feel feverish. Just suddenly—(*He snaps his fingers.*) Like that.

ELEANOR. You get into bed. (*Crosses* U.L.) I'll bring you up a tray.

FDR. (*Crosses to stairs.*) (*With a half smile.*) I hoped you'd say that. (*Just as FDR reaches the landing the voices of the children can be heard. Eleanor and FDR stop.*)

CHILDREN. (*Off.*) Two, four, six, eight, who do we appreciate? Mrs. McGowan, Mrs. McGowan, Mrs. McGowan. (*Sounds of clapping and yells. FDR and Eleanor exchange a grin. Then she goes into the dining room and FDR, alone, walks heavily up the steps.*)

CURTAIN

PROPERTY PLOT

Act I, Scene 1 to Act I, Scene 2

Strike and Set

Strike:

Letters from Table U.L.
Newspapers from chaise
Glass from in front of chaise
Megaphone
Scotch bottle from closet
Croquet mallets from window seat
Sailboat from window sill R.
Puzzle from table U.C.
Volume of Shakespeare from
   window seat
2 paddles from umbrella stand
All clothing from umbrella stand
   except original

2 pieces
Pennant and rope from chaise
Sewing basket from table D.C.

Set:

Dominoes Table D.C.L. side
Newspapers R. of Table D.C. on floor
Newspapers on Table D.C.L. side
Lamp from Table U.C. to Table D.C.
   and plug switch on Lamp Table
   U.L.
Howe's coat on chair L. of Table D.C.
Window U.R. down
Unspring door U.L.C.

Preset for Act I, Scene 2

Furniture the same as Act I, Scene 1

Off L. *Table:*

Catheterizing set on tray—ELEANOR
Book—JAMES
Tray containing:—ELEANOR
   3 cups
   3 saucers

3 napkins
3 spoons
Saucer of lemon
Teapot
Creamer
Sugar
Cigarettes and matches—HOWE

20

ACT ONE

Scene Two

The scene is the same. It is September first. It is night. Kerosene lamps dimly illuminate the room. At rise Louis Howe enters from the kitchen D.R. *with a tray covered with a white napkin. He hurries upstairs.*

ELEANOR'S VOICE. (*Offstage upstairs.*) Louie—

HOWE. Be right there.

ELEANOR'S VOICE. (*Offstage.*) Thank you, Louie. (*Jimmy enters from side room* U.L. *and crosses to stairs.*)

HOWE. Call me if you need anything. (*He comes down the steps and sees Jimmy. During the above Jimmy has crossed to the bottom of the stairs wearing pajamas and bathrobe.*) Hello, Jim. What's wrong?

JIMMY. (*At stairs.*) Nothing, Mr. Howe.

HOWE. Then why aren't you asleep?

JIMMY. I couldn't sleep. How's my father?

HOWE. Having a fairly good night. (*Crosses* D.L.C.)

JIMMY. Can I see him?

HOWE. No . . . in a couple of days.

JIMMY. We're all a little scared.

HOWE. (*In a reprimanding tone.*) Well your father isn't and he wouldn't want you to be, Jim.

JIMMY. I'll try. I'd feel better if I knew what was going on, (*Crosses* C.) but I don't want to bother Mother.

HOWE. That's right. She's had enough to do for the past three weeks.

JIMMY. But—

HOWE. But what?

JIMMY. Sometimes I get frightened. So does Anna.

HOWE. Well stop being frightened. Those germs never ran into anybody as tough as your father. They'll be yelling for help by the time he gets through with them. (*Jimmy crosses* L. *to sofa.*)

21

JIMMY. He's strong all right. (*Crosses* D.L., *sits on couch.*)

HOWE. (*Now placatingly.*) (*Crosses* D.L., *sits on couch with Jimmy.*) He's a strong and big man in many ways. Jimmy, when I first got up here I was scared too. I was worried about your father being so sick, but now he's beginning to fight back—and when he fights—well, you know, the first time I saw your father was in Albany in 1911. He was fighting a tough battle with Tammany Hall and those fellows can fight like roughnecks. Well, he won that one going away—like what Dempsey did to Carpentier. And Jimmy, he's going to win this one.

JIMMY. (*Relieved.*) I hope you're right.

HOWE. (*Rises and crosses* C.) I've never been wrong in my life. Only once when I figured the ice on the pond in Saratoga was thick enough to skate on. Well sir, it took them three days to wring me out. (*Picks up newspaper from table* D.C.) (*Eleanor, carrying a tray, appears on the stairs. Jimmy and Howe turn as she appears.*)

ELEANOR. (*As she sees Jimmy.*) Jimmy— (*Jimmy rises.*)

JIMMY. (*Crosses to stairs.*) I was just up for a glass of water, mother. (*Jimmy takes tray and exits to the kitchen* D.R.)

ELEANOR. Thank you.

HOWE. All right? (*Eleanor nods, as she takes off her apron. Jimmy returns from the kitchen.*)

HOWE. Eleanor, why the hell can't we get some electric lights in here?

ELEANOR. Now, Louie, you know we can't. All right, dear. Now you go in and get some sleep.

JIMMY. I will. And you'd better get some rest too, Mother. (*Eleanor nods.*) 'Night.

ELEANOR. Good night, James.

JIMMY. Good night, Mr. Howe.

HOWE. Good night, Jimmy. (*Jimmy exits into the side room* U.L.)

ELEANOR. Now, Louie, what's bothering you?

HOWE. Where's Mrs. Roosevelt?

ELEANOR. (*Crosses* C., *sits.*) Mama is in her room. She'll probably be down in a few minutes. Louie, be understanding. This has been a desperately unhappy day for her.

HOWE. (*Crosses* L.C.) I am understanding, Eleanor. I like the

22

old lady. She fascinates me. Monumental and impregnable like the Rock of Gibraltar.

ELEANOR. I know your problem with Mama.

HOWE. (*Crosses* R.C.) It's no problem. She just hates the sight of me. She considers me the ward heeler in Franklin's life. (*Rises.*)

ELEANOR. (*Crosses* D.R., *sits.*) Please don't quarrel with her.

HOWE. Eleanor, I promise to shinny on my side if she shinnies on hers.

ELEANOR. Louie.

HOWE. (*Crosses* D.R.) *Mein Gott*, it's going to be rough, Eleanor, but you're going to have to tell her the truth.

ELEANOR. Oh, Louie. He should be in a hospital, getting the best care, the most modern treatment. If only we can get him well enough to move him into New York.

HOWE. Now you must remember this: nobody could have done more than you or done it better.

SARA. (*Off.*) Eleanor? Franklin sleeping? (*Sara enters from stairs.*)

ELEANOR. (*Crosses* U.L.) (*Howe crosses to* D.L.C. *chair, takes coat off back of chair, puts it on as he crosses* U.L.) Yes, he's been resting for over two hours.

SARA. Has the pain eased?

ELEANOR. A bit. His legs are less sensitive to touch. A cup of tea, mama?

SARA. Yes, I would like a cup.

ELEANOR. Only be a moment. (*Exits* D.R.)

HOWE. How are you feeling, Mrs. Roosevelt?

SARA. (*Crosses* U.R.) Oh, Mr. Howe. A little tired, but a good night's rest will pick me up, I'm sure. I came up directly from New York after the ship docked. The crossing was rather rough and seemed endless.

HOWE. (*Crosses* R.C.) Yes, so Eleanor said.

SARA. How is your wife?

HOWE. Thank you, Grace is fine. She took my son Hartley home yesterday.

SARA. The air is rather stuffy, don't you think?

HOWE. (*Crosses* L.C.) We had the door open but it's damn cold outside.

23

SARA. Have you been here all the time since Franklin's illness?

HOWE. I got here a couple of days after he took ill. Been here since, and plan to stay till we take him back.

SARA. Do the doctors know when that will be?

HOWE. They hope in a couple of weeks.

SARA. (*Crosses* c.) I admire the way all of you are behaving. (*Eleanor enters* D.R.)

ELEANOR. (*Crosses* U.L.C.) Louie, tea?

HOWE. No, thanks.

SARA. Eleanor, dear, I hope you're not too worn out, because this is the first opportunity we've had to talk.

ELEANOR. Yes, mama—

HOWE. Mrs. Roosevelt, this girl has worked like a whole squad of trained nurses. Dr. Lovett was amazed at how well she's been able to do it all.

SARA. (*Sits* c.) Couldn't you get any nurses, dear?

ELEANOR. (*Crosses to Sara.*) We tried, but none were available. Campobello is quite remote.

SARA. If you don't mind, I'm anxious to hear as much as I can about everything.

ELEANOR. (*Crosses* D.R. *gets ottoman, crosses* c., *sits.*) Franklin was taken ill just three weeks ago. At first it appeared to be a heavy cold. Finally, Dr. Bennet called in a specialist who diagnosed it as a clot on the spinal cord.

SARA. He couldn't have been a good specialist.

ELEANOR. We thought he was. But Franklin didn't respond to the treatment. About a week ago, Uncle Fred reached me by telephone—we have to go into town for that.

SARA. I always thought it was absurd to be so cut off.

ELEANOR. You know Franklin never wanted a telephone up here.

SARA. Go ahead, dear.

ELEANOR. Uncle Fred had talked to some other doctors who began to suspect it was infantile paralysis. So he arranged for Dr. Lovett of Boston to come up. He diagnosed it almost immediately, and we're doing as he suggested ever since.

SARA. And what does he think? How severe is the paralysis?

ELEANOR. He believes it to be a mild attack, and feels that Franklin will recover almost completely.

24

SARA. Almost—?

ELEANOR. Well, mama, at first Franklin lost control even of his hands. He couldn't write or hold a spoon. Now his arms and hands are almost all well. We still don't know about his back or his legs.

SARA. —he can't sit up?

ELEANOR. No, dear, not yet. (*Sara puts down her cup, takes a handkerchief and puts it to her lips, stifling a desire to cry.*)

HOWE. The doctors feel sure his back muscles will be all right.

SARA. His legs, those wonderful legs—what about them?

ELEANOR. The doctors don't know.

SARA. It's too much. I can't believe it. My poor boy—

ELEANOR. (*Rises, crosses C.*) Mama, perhaps we shouldn't talk any more. You're exhausted.

SARA. No, I couldn't sleep right now. The children—is it safe for them to be here?

ELEANOR. Dr. Lovett said, having already been exposed to the illness, there's no point in moving them.

SARA. I can certainly help with the children.

ELEANOR. Mama, that would be wonderful.

HOWE. (*Rises.*) Eleanor, you have to get some rest. We all do. I think I'll turn in, myself. Excuse me?

SARA. Goodnight, Mr. Howe.

ELEANOR. Rest well, Louie.

HOWE. (*Crosses to stairs, stumbles. Eleanor crosses to him.*) Night. I don't know why the hell they can't put some electric light in here. (*Exits upstairs, wheezing and coughing and smoking.*)

SARA. He's a vulgar little man.

ELEANOR. (*Crosses D.L.C.*) He's a very dear little man.

SARA. I find him very difficult.

ELEANOR. You make that quite clear.

SARA. I'm not skillful at hiding my true feelings, Eleanor.

ELEANOR. (*Sits D.L.C.*) That may not be a virtue, mama. You should know that as soon as Louie heard of Franklin's illness, he gave up a lucrative job in Washington to rush here and help out. There's nothing in life more important to him than Franklin.

SARA. Nor to any of us.

ELEANOR. Then that is something we can share with Louie, isn't it?

25

SARA. It has been a gruelling day. I'm tired.

ELEANOR. Mama, there's something very special in the relationship between Louie and Franklin.

SARA. (*Rises, crosses* U.R.C.) I've never quite understood it. It's possible Mr. Howe merely enjoys riding along on Franklin's coat tails.

HOWE. (*Off.*) Eleanor.

ELEANOR. Yes, Louie. (*Howe enters on stairs.*)

HOWE. Franklin needs you for a minute. (*Eleanor hurries upstairs. Sara starts to follow, but is stopped by Howe.*)

SARA. Eleanor?

HOWE. (*Crosses* D.L.) It's nothing alarming, Mrs. Roosevelt.

SARA. You suffer a great deal from asthma, don't you?

HOWE. (*As he lights a cigarette.*) A great deal. I'd be lonesome without it.

SARA. You know that smoking isn't very good for it, you know that?

HOWE. I do. (*He puffs deliberately in defiance of Sara's advice.*)

SARA. What are the plans for Franklin after he is taken to New York?

HOWE. Well, first he goes to the hospital for treatments, and then —well, I guess it depends on how all that goes.

SARA. You say he'll be able to be moved in two or three weeks?

HOWE. We hope so.

SARA. (*Crosses* D.R.C., *sits.*) As soon as Franklin is able to leave the hospital I want him to go to Hyde Park. Everything he loves is there. It's home to him, always has been. It's large enough for the entire family, and that's where he can be made most comfortable.

HOWE. (*Crosses* D.L.C.) Well, I'm sure that as soon as Franklin is well enough, he and Eleanor will decide where he wants to recuperate.

SARA. If Franklin has any permanent injury, the best place for him is Hyde Park. We can make a full life for him there. He can write, take care of the estate, raise his family as he was raised. There will be enough to keep him active without overtaxing him or spending his energy.

HOWE. (*Crosses* D.R.) Mrs. Roosevelt, I have heard Franklin say

26

that in public service a man must be prepared to spend and be spent. He may not be willing to accept a sedentary life in the country.

SARA. Mr. Howe, you must do everything possible to discourage him from trying to remain in politics.

HOWE. Permanent injury or not—Hyde Park or Timbuctu—Franklin's political future is ordained. (*Crosses* D.L.C.) That sounds mystical, I know. But I feel it as sure as I feel my heart beating.

SARA. Believe me, Mr. Howe, I respect your devotion, but Franklin is more to me than a prospective candidate for public office. He's my son.

HOWE. But he is also Eleanor's husband, the father of five children, and my dearest friend.

SARA. Then he is blessed indeed to be the subject of so much affection.

HOWE. But he's above all himself, and he happens to be the best damned progressive in the country.

SARA. (*Rises.*) My only interest is in his getting well, not in his status as a politician.

HOWE. Mrs. Roosevelt.

SARA. I am grateful for the care and devotion you have given Franklin. I will be less grateful for your untimely and grandiose schemes.

HOWE. For the next few months, Franklin may have need of some grandiose schemes. So may we all.

SARA. Goodnight, Mr. Howe. (*She starts upstairs* R.)

CURTAIN

PROPERTY PLOT

ACT I, SCENE 2 to ACT I, SCENE 3

Strike and Set

Strike:

Tea service from Table D.C.
Lamp from Table D.C. to Table U.C.
Newspapers from Table D.C. and area

Set:

Table and 2 chairs D.C. to 13 marks
Ottoman to 13 marks
Sea bag against windowseat
Howe's briefcase Table U.C.
Howe's hat—Umbrella stand
Typewriter open with paper in it
    Table D.R.
Typewriter lid in chair above
    Table D.R.
3 pieces of luggage on ottoman
2 pieces of luggage on landing and
    1st step of staircase respectively
Golf bag moves to D.L. end of chaise
File box open lid U.S. below chaise
Tennis racquet on stage end of chaise
Sail boat offstage end of chaise
Window U.L. open
Door U.L.C. open and hooked back

Prop Table off R.

Feather on headring—JOHNNY
Bow and arrows—JOHNNY

Prop Table off L.

Suitcase—HOWE
News Release—HOWE
Straw hat box—ANNA
Doctor's bag and hat—DR. BENNET
Stretcher—MEN
Blanket for stretcher—FDR
Leather handbag containing house
    keys and handkerchief—ELEANOR
Blanket—ELEANOR
"Get Well" letters in manila
    envelope—ELEANOR
FDR's hat—ELEANOR
Dog—DR. BENNET
Baseball mitt—ELEANOR
Black vanity bag—SARA
Cigarettes and holder in pocket of
    FDR's robe
Matches—HOWE
Watch—HOWE

28

ACT ONE

Scene Three

We are in the living room again. There is some luggage stacked around. It is a sunny morning, September 13, 1921.

Missy LeHand sits at the table R., typing from some notes. She is FDR's private secretary. She is a handsome woman, with auburn hair and a strong and sure manner. Edward enters D.R., followed by Johnny, who carries a bow and arrow and wears a simple Indian headdress. As Johnny comes in, he lets out an Indian war whoop.

EDWARD. (*Crosses to suitcases U.R.C.*) Mr. Johnny, I'm busy. I can't play Indians any more. (*Johnny crosses to suitcases D.S. of Edward.*) It's not your work. Now you go about your business and let me go about mine. (*Edward exits U.L.C. with suitcases.*)
MISSY. How, Great Chief! Need anything?
JOHNNY (c.) Just Anna. Jimmy sent me in for her. He orders us around like we were in the Navy. (*Crosses to stairs.*) (*Calling out.*) Anna!
MISSY. Sh!
JOHNNY. Sorry. Anna!
ANNA. (*From upstairs.*) Ssh. (*She appears on stairs, carrying her suitcase and coat. She is dressed for departure.*) Stop yelling like a wild Indian.
JOHNNY. (*Crosses c.*) Jimmy says—
ANNA. (*She has come down the stairs, crosses to ottoman and puts her bag and coat down.*) What Jimmy says doesn't interest me in the slightest.
JOHNNY. We're supposed to wait outside.
ANNA. (*At c., fixing hair ribbon.*) I know. Like children.
JOHNNY. I enjoy being a boy.
ANNA. I'm going to have some breakfast and then go out the back way. (*Exits D.R. with her bag and coat.*)

29

JOHNNY. Miss LeHand, they gonna carry father out on a stretcher?

MISSY. (*Crosses, sits* D.L.) That's the plan.

JOHNNY. (*Crosses* D.L.) Why can't Jimmy, Elliott, Franklin and I do it?

MISSY. That's a wonderful idea. But your father has made other plans and it's too late to change.

JOHNNY. Okay. I'd better go before Jimmy sends Elliott for me. (*Howe enters from stairs, carrying a suitcase.*) Good morning, Mr. Howe. (*Exits* D.R.)

MISSY. He's a cute one.

HOWE. (*Leaves his bag at foot of stairs, crosses* D.L.) They're all cute, but there's sure a hell of a lot of them. How's it going, Missy?

MISSY. Well now that Anna is downstairs the kids are all packed and waiting for the Robert E. Lee.

HOWE. Mama?

MISSY. Upstairs with the boss and Mrs. R. Doc Bennet, too.

HOWE. We've got about an hour.

MISSY. This is going to be a rough trip for Mr. R.

HOWE. Once we get him across the bay and into Eastport, the rough time's over.

MISSY. (*Rises, crosses* D.R.) Oh, you're going to have a lot of angry newspapermen breathing down your collar. They all want to see Mr. R.

HOWE. (*Crosses* D.R.C.) They'll see him, after we get him on the train, all propped up in his berth, with a grin on his face. Once we get to Eastport I'll flash the other dock, then tell the newspapermen to come over, and say there was a change of plans due to the tides or the currents or something.

MISSY. (*Crosses* D.R.C.) Well, when do we break the story that the boss has infantile?

HOWE. (*Crosses* D.R.) (*Takes news release from pocket.*) Later. After we get him to New York. Some time tomorrow. "After thorough examinations, doctors today revealed Franklin D. Roosevelt recently suffered from a mild attack of infantile paralysis. His legs are temporarily affected but it is anticipated he will have a complete recovery."

30

MISSY. Well, here's a gay little news item.

HOWE. Missy, where are those usual radiantly hopeful thoughts?

MISSY. (D.L., *sits.*) Louie—I've been here for two weeks taking dictation and trying to act like he does, as if nothing is the matter. Sometimes it seems like a sad and foolish game.

HOWE. (*Crosses,* D.R.) Missy.

MISSY. I'm sorry. He lies there rattling on with plans for business conferences and meetings. Overhaul the Democratic party, select the candidates for twenty-two and twenty-four, organize this charity, and reorganize that. (*Rises, crosses* D.R.) I listen with wonder and want to cry.

HOWE. (*Crosses to Missy.*) Now listen to me. Maybe he doesn't mean one word of what he's planning or trying to do. But he wants us to believe it. So, believe.

MISSY. Yes, Louie.

HOWE. (*Edward enters* U.L.C.) Edward, my stuff goes into the boat headed to Eastport.

EDWARD. Yes sir, I know. (*Picks up bag at foot of stair, crosses to window seat, gets bag.*) What about your things, Miss LeHand?

MISSY. Oh, to the first boat, thank you, Edward. (*Edward exits* U.L.C.) (*Dr. Bennet enters from stairs.*)

BENNET. (*Crosses* U.L.) Well, our patient's about ready to be moved. I'll send the men in with the stretcher. When they bring Mr. Roosevelt down, we'll give them a short rest in here and then take him to the boat.

MISSY. Doctor, how is he today?

BENNET. (*Crosses* U.L.C.) About the same. He's in pain, but I've given him something to help that. He's also running a fever, but he refuses to take it seriously. Body of a bull, disposition of a lamb. (*He crosses to door* U.L.C., *Goes out to porch.*) (*Sara enters on stairs.*)

HOWE. Good morning, Mrs. Roosevelt.

SARA. (*On stairs.*) Good morning. Are the children all ready, Miss LeHand?

MISSY. Yes, they're all outside.

SARA. I don't think they should see their father carried out on a stretcher. Therefore—

HOWE. Well —That may be unavoidable. . . .

31

MISSY. Certainly the least excitement for Mr. Roosevelt the better. (*Edward enters* U.L.C. *for last few pieces of luggage.*)

EDWARD. Is this everything?

MISSY. I think so, Edward. (*Dr. Bennet and stretcher bearers enter* U.L.C., *carrying a stretcher.*)

HOWE. (*Crosses* U.R.C.) Good morning, men.

CALDER. (*The leader of the group.*) Morning, Sir. Ma'am. (*The others nod as they remove their hats.*)

MISSY. Morning.

HOWE. Gentlemen, I want to thank all of you sincerely for what you have done and are doing.

CALDER. No thanks expected, Mr. Howe.

BENNET. Look at the stretcher they made. They even fixed up a back rest.

HOWE. Wonderful, really.

BENNET. We'd better move. (*As the men are directed upstairs by Dr. Bennet, who precedes them, Edward exits* U.L.C. *Sara looks upstairs apprehensively. Eleanor comes down from upstairs. She carries her large handbag, an extra blanket, a soft felt hat of FDR's and a manila envelope.*)

MEN. (*As they pass her.*) Morning, ma'am!

ELEANOR. (*Crosses* D.R.) Good morning, Captain Calder. (*Handing Missy an envelope.*) Missy, these are some get well letters which came in before you arrived. I had no time to answer.

MISSY. Small wonder. (*She puts envelope in briefcase.*)

ELEANOR. Are the children all ready?

MISSY. Yes. Mademoiselle is with them near the dock.

SARA. I don't think the children should see this.

ELEANOR. (*Crosses* U.R.) They may have to learn to see a lot of things.

SARA. Perhaps. But it may be a shock. Particularly to the younger ones.

HOWE. They'll get older.

SARA. Mr. Howe.

HOWE. I didn't mean that the way it sounded, but I think Eleanor's right. (*Eleanor crosses* D.R.)

SARA. I believe you and I have varying opinions of what is right and wrong.

32

ELEANOR. Frankly, I suppose the children are excited by it. They'd probably love to be carried to a boat on a stretcher.

SARA. Furthermore, Franklin's departure must not be handled like a circus.

ELEANOR. (*Crosses* U.L.R. *then crosses* D.L. *for props, tennis racquets, etc.*) Mama, Franklin is a man of some reputation. We can't give an imperial order to ask the crowds to disperse.

HOWE. I think you must agree, Mrs. Roosevelt, that it is far better to have the ubiquitous press first find Franklin sitting up in his berth on the train, than see him carried on a stretcher.

SARA. Franklin's day of departure could have been kept a secret.

HOWE. No, it couldn't. *Mein Gott!* (*Sara crosses to stairs.*) Mrs. Roosevelt, the press has been eyeing Campobello since the day Franklin took ill.

ELEANOR. Mama, I, too, have seen him run up and down these steps many times—

SARA. (*Crosses* C.) I do not approve of Franklin being placed on exhibition.

ELEANOR. This is not a pleasant day for any of us—particularly Franklin. (*She crosses to stairs. The stretcher bearers appear at top of stairs, guided by Dr. Bennet. On the stretcher is FDR. He wears a plain dark-blue robe over pajamas and is partly covered by blankets.*)

BENNET. (*As the men carry FDR downstairs.*) Lift your side— right. That's it. Now lower the other side. Fine. Now over the post. (*Stretcher bearers bring stretcher down safely.*)

FDR. Men, it's a lot easier going down than up. Be grateful for small favors. (*Sara, Eleanor, Howe, and Missy watch. Sara grips her pocketbook, Missy stands tense, and Eleanor, holding the brim of FDR's hat, fingers it nervously. The men set the stretcher on the floor* D.C.) Thank you, gentlemen. The journey was a pleasant one. Where's my missus?

ELEANOR. (*Crosses to FDR.*) Here I am, darling.

FDR. How about a look around, Doc?

BENNET. Yes indeed. (*With Eleanor and Calder Dr. Bennet props up back of stretcher so that FDR can sit up, look around. Dr. Bennet ushers the men out, indicating that he will call them when ready.*)

FDR. I tell you, there's no other way to travel. (*He digs into his robe, produces a pack of cigarettes and his holder. Peers around.*) The place hasn't changed in the month I've been away. (*Howe steps over to him, lights his cigarette.*) Thanks, Louie, my boy. How have you planned the logistics?

HOWE. (D.L. *of stretcher.*) Well, first the children, Missy, your mother, and Eleanor take off for the main dock. That's where the sight-seers and the press are congregated. A goodly crowd has gathered and waits eagerly. (*Kneels, goes into a heavy Dutch burlesque accent.*) But, *mein herr*, vile all der peoples is vatching der vun boat coming on der water, ve go avay in der oder boat for Eastport, und get on der train. *Gut, nicht war?*

FDR. Ah, a diversionary tactic.

HOWE. Precisely, *mein herr.*

FDR. As assistant secretary of the Navy I used to rate a seventeen gun salute. Have you arranged for that?

HOWE. You're just an ex-assistant. No guns. You're lucky we got water.

FDR. Eleanor, you'd better give me that hat before you tear it to ribbons. (*Eleanor crosses to FDR, gives him hat, which he puts on his head.*) How do I look, snappy?

SARA. Never better.

FDR. Louie, I approve of your plan.

HOWE. It's about time. I've been waiting breathlessly.

FDR. He's not fooling. Louie's first love was the theater. He loves applause. (*Louie does time step.*)

HOWE. (*Looks at his watch.*) I hate to break up the party, but I think boat number one ought to be on its way.

MISSY. That's me.

FDR. Missy, plan coming to the hospital Thursday morning. Will you have everything typed by then?

MISSY. (*Crosses* U.L.C.) Of course.

FDR. Fine. What's the date of the Boy Scout dinner?

MISSY. The seventh of November.

FDR. We'd better cancel that. I don't know if I'll feel up to making speeches until after the New Year.

MISSY. Right.

FDR. And bring the list of conferences I had to cancel because of this ridiculous child's disease and we'll plan some new dates.

BENNET. That's all, Franklin. They have to get started. You can do all that on the train.

SARA. We'll be on our way before they bring you out?

FDR. I expect so, mama.

SARA. I'll tell the children that they'll see you on the train.

FDR. Bon voyage, mama.

SARA. (*Gives him a kiss.*) Bon voyage.

MISSY. See you, boss. (*FDR waves a farewell as Sara and Missy leave* U.L.C.)

FDR. Well, the party is thinning out. (*He removes his hat and rubs his hand through his hair absently.*) I think I can say the same for my hair. Where's Duffy?

ELEANOR. (*Crosses to FDR.*) Outside waiting for us.

FDR. Babs, please bring him in. Let him ride with me.

BENNET. (*Crosses out* U.L.C. *for "Duffy." Eleanor follows him to doorway.*) No harm in it. I'll get him.

FDR. Well, Louie, I must say you look wretched.

HOWE. You know how I hate sea travel.

FDR. You could get rid of your asthma if you'd breathe in some good sea air and cut out those cigarettes.

HOWE. Look who the hell's talking about cigarettes.

FDR. I haven't got asthma.

HOWE. *Touché!* (*Bennet enters* U.L.C. *with Duffy, a black Scottie, gives Duffy to Eleanor at door. She carries him in, hands him to FDR.*)

FDR. Hello, Duffy, you old pirate. Say, you're getting fat. One of these days I'll have to take you for a long run in the woods. (*Edward enters* U.L.C.)

EDWARD. (*Crosses* U.R.C.) We're ready to go, Mrs. Roosevelt.

BENNET. It's time.

ELEANOR. (*Digs into her bag for some keys.*) These are the keys, Edward. You lock up when you make the return trip.

EDWARD. Yes ma'am, I'll get everything shipshape.

ELEANOR. Drain the pipes.

EDWARD. (*Crosses* D.L.) And board up the windows until next season.

35

HOWE. I'll walk you to the boat, Eleanor. See you on the dock, Franklin. (*He exits* U.L.C.)

EDWARD. Goodbye, Mr. Roosevelt. And good luck to you, sir.

FDR. Thank you, Edward. (*Edward exits* U.L.C.)

BENNET. I'll be with the men, Franklin. (*Exits* U.L.C.)

ELEANOR. Franklin, I'm to cross with the children.

FDR. How's the sea today?

ELEANOR. (*Crosses to FDR.*) Choppy.

FDR. West wind?

ELEANOR. That's right.

FDR. Calder handling the boat?

ELEANOR. Yes.

FDR. He's a good man.

ELEANOR. I'll call the men. (*Eleanor walks to the* U.L.C. *door to wave the men in. As she leaves, FDR sags back against the stretcher. Suddenly we are aware of what a strain this has been for him. He looks weary and tired. He lowers his head and then looks up and looks around the room as a wave of memories flood his mind. His hands drop in fatigue and pain, and he releases his hat, which he has been holding. It falls out of his reach. As he attempts to retrieve it, we see that he cannot move his back. His fingers stretch for it but he cannot touch it. He breathes heavily. Eleanor returns* U.L.C. *and, realizing what has happened, hands him his hat. Dr. Bennet returns* U.L.C. *with the men, and FDR pulls himself together.*)

ELEANOR. Franklin, are you sure you can manage this trip?

FDR. I'm going to make a damn good try, Babs. (*Eleanor blows a kiss, FDR puts his hat on, lifts it to her, and puts his cigarette holder in his mouth in that familiar perky fashion. He holds Duffy in one arm. The men reach down and lift the stretcher.*)

DR. BENNET. All right men— (*They start out.*)

FDR. Gentlemen—thank you for the sedan chair. (*As he is carried out* U.L.C.) By gosh—I feel like the Caliph of Bagdad.

CURTAIN

PROPERTY PLOT

Act II

Furniture:

Bridge Table D.R.C.
Armchair L. of Bridge Table
Utility Table U.R.C. behind sofa
End Table U.R.C., above sofa
Armchair U.L.C.
End Table above armchair U.L.C.
Desk L.
Ottoman D.C.
Wheelchair R.C. behind bridge table
Straightback chair U.L.C. against case
Coalscuttle L. of fireplace
Fire tongs R. of fireplace
Fire screen
2 Andirons
Fire effect
Pedestal L. above window

Decorative Dressing

Case of birds on wall above D.R. door
Bust on Bookcase above D.R. door
2 pictures—wall U.R.
1 picture on Bookcase U.R.
Books in all cases
Diplomas and Group Pictures—
  U.R.C. wall
Sailing ship—Bookcase U.R.C.
3 Books on top of bookcase U.R.C.,
  R. of mantel
Portrait of James Roosevelt above
  mantel
Clock on mantel
2 un-practical hurricane lamps
  on mantel
Portrait of ships and group pictures
  on wall U.L.C.

1 Sailing ship—Bookcase U.L.C.
1 Sailing ship—on top of books on
  top of bookcase U.L.C.
1 large vase on top of pedestal L.
Drapes and curtains on window L.
Envelope holder with envelopes on
  Desk L.

On Stage Props

4 Personal letters—bridge table
  D.R.C.—MISSY
2 Packets of stamps one with corner
  turned up, Bridge Table
1 Magnifying glass, Bridge Table R.
1 Stamp Album—Bridge Table R.
1 Stamp Album—Floor R. of Bridge
  Table
1 open Stamp album R. end of Sofa
1 half-finished boat model on utility
  table
Wood shavings and pieces of sails
  on Utility Table and in ashtray
  and on floor R. of Utility Table
Gold framed picture—Utility Table
Child's fairy tales on top of bookcase U.L.
Tweezers (a gadget with an exten-
  sion arm which when expanded
  reaches to the floor) on D.R. corner
  of desk L.
Cigarette Box with 1 cigarette, box
  of wooden matches, ashtray—
  Desk L.
Pen set—Desk L.
1 Pillow on chair D.R.
1 Pillow on L. side of sofa

3 pencils—L. top drawer of desk

Papers and Folder—L. bottom drawer of desk. In folder: Grocery bill and odd papers

Lamp on Utility Table U.R.C.—L. side

Lamp on Desk L.—U.R. side

Offstage R.

6 Letters with envelopes attached (Polio victims) Fresh each evening (MISSY) in stack

1 pile of letters (6) Forestry letter on top

Double spaced Cordell Hull letter and four fresh letters with envelopes attached (MISSY)

Missy's briefcase containing papers, notepad and fountain pen (MISSY)

Penned letter from Jimmy—ELEANOR

Typed letter from Woodrow Wilson —ELEANOR

3 Books with straps—FDR JR.

Stack of newspapers, Chicago Tribune—HOWE

List of Clubs—HOWE

Briefcase with Brimmer's special material: *Note:* Double Howe's case from 13—BRIMMER

2 Books—ELEANOR

Cloth sail—ELEANOR

Old leg braces—to be set

Crutches—to be set

Offstage L.

3 letters with attached envelopes— to be set 22

6 letters on colored stationery with envelopes—to be set

Letter from Montracol Oil Co.—to be set

ACT TWO
Scene 1

It is May, 1922. Curtain reveals the downstage living room of the New York House on 65th Street. Like all the Roosevelt homes it is warm and tasteful and not at all pretentious.

At D.R. *is the door to Missy's office. Upstage in the* R. *wall are double French doors leading to the rest of the house. The rear wall is lined with bookshelves, with a fireplace in the center of the wall.* D.R. *is a bridge table, with FDR's wheelchair (a converted kitchen chair)* R. *of it, and an armchair* L.U.C., *placed at a slant, is the sofa, with a utility table behind it and an end table upstage of the sofa. An ottoman at* C. *well downstage. An armchair is* L.C. *with an end table above it. (The end tables flank each side of the fireplace.) A straight-back chair stands against the bookcase at* L. *A desk stands downstage at* L.

FDR is seen D.R. *sitting at bridge table in one of his small kitchen chairs converted for him into a wheel chair. He is working on some stamps. He glues a stamp in the book, then reaching for the packet of stamps accidentally knocks it off the table. He looks around, frowns, then scoots his chair over to a desk on the other side of the room for his "tweezers." He scoots back to the bridge table and, using the gadget, picks up the stamps. He is already quite expert at wheeling his chair. His attitude is far from cheerful.*

Missy enters D.R. *from office next to the living room. She carries a sheaf of letters for FDR to sign. She, like the others who are close to FDR, is sensitive to his moods and so she is aware that FDR is having one of his rare bad days.*

MISSY. (*Crosses to bridge table* L. *of FDR.*) Sorry, boss, to interrupt, but you wanted to get these off. I still have those letters Louie dictated. I hope to finish them before I go tonight. (*FDR pushes his stamps away and places letters on the table.*) In the letter to the Park Commission I may have made a mistake. I couldn't remember whether you said sixty thousand trees or sixteen. (*FDR is reading letters.*)

FDR. (*Not looking up.*) Sixteen.

MISSY. Good. That's what I typed in.

FDR. My enunciation is usually precise enough to make the distinction between sixteen and sixty.

MISSY. No criticism, Mr. R. My hearing must be failing.

FDR. (*Handing her a letter.*) You'll have to correct this. It's Pinehenge Farm, not Pinhenge. (*Missy takes it, looks at it. FDR refers to next letter.*) Missy, this rough draft of the letter to Cordell Hull should be triple spaced.

MISSY. (*Ruefully.*) I'm having a good day.

FDR. Well, if you must know, I'm having a perfectly wretched day.

MISSY. I'm sorry.

FDR. I can't wear the leg braces because they don't fit. And I don't know why I'm going all the way to Boston to get new ones that also won't fit. And I'm fed up with all those friendly hints that come in the mail—everything from ancient nostrums to brand new gadgets invented by people all the way from Keokuk to Zanzibar.

MISSY. (*Crosses to* D.R. *door.*) They all want to help, not hurt.

FDR. Oh, Missy, stop it. No sweetness and light today, please. (*Refers to letters.*) Take them away. (*Eleanor enters through French doors* U.R. *She carries books and letters.*)

ELEANOR. Franklin, I've talked to Regan. He's arranged for the railroad trip to Boston.

FDR. (*Crosses to desk* D.L.) I may not go to Boston.

ELEANOR. Well, you don't have to go until Friday. You can decide by then. (*Crosses to FDR. at desk, hands him the mail.*) There's a cheery letter from Jimmy. And one from Woodrow Wilson.

FDR. (*Reading the letter.*) I'm glad to read that Jimmy anticipates good marks. Well, that's a relief—he loves Groton. I'm sure Groton is relieved to. (*He picks up the one from Woodrow Wilson. Eleanor is putting the books away. Missy glances at the letters she has picked up from FDR's table. FDR reads Wilson's letter, his mood changing a bit.*) It's an extremely considerate note.

40

(*Reads.*) "I am indeed glad to hear that you are getting so well and so confidently, and I shall try and be generous enough not to envy you. I hope that your generous labors in behalf of the Wilson Foundation have not overtaxed you, and you are certainly to be congratulated on your successful leadership in the complicated and difficult undertaking." Really quite thoughtful of him.

ELEANOR. You have done a lot for the Foundation.

FDR. Only because I believe in it. Either we develop some plan for world peace and order or the world will chop itself into bits.

MISSY. Excuse me, boss, may I get on with the rest of these?

FDR. (*Cheerier.*) On your way, Missy. Later I want to do another draft of that letter to Cordell Hull. What I've got is too obscure. Sixteen. (*Missy exits* D.R.) I was apologizing for having lost my temper.

ELEANOR. (*Crosses* D.R. *to table.*) I had a rather tense chore a few minutes ago. I had to let the upstairs maid go. She complained so much about all the work she had to do—most of which she never did anyway.

FDR. (*Crosses* D.R. *to table.*) Sorry, Babs. You've had a big turnover on maids this year. It's been a busy household.

ELEANOR. It's been a nice household.

FDR. (*Crosses* D.L. *to desk. Puts some of his things away.*) (*Eleanor crosses* U.L.) I'm getting expert with this chair. It moves easily. See that? We have to get a couple like these for Hyde Park. None of those conventional invalid wheel chairs. (*He takes another turn or two in his chair.*) This exercise is stimulating. Takes some of that loneliness away. (*Crosses* C. *to couch and picks up sailboat on table behind sofa.*)

ELEANOR. (*Crosses to couch.*) Loneliness, dear?

FDR. Invalidism, (*quickly*) even temporary, is very lonely. I remember reading, "A sick man wishes to be where he is not." When you're forced to sit a lot and watch others move around, you feel apart, lonely, because you can't get up and pace around. I find myself irritated when people come in and parade all over the place. I have to keep exercising self-control to prevent screaming at them to sit down, quiet down, stand still.

ELEANOR. I'll remember. (*Crosses* D.R.C., *moves table* U.S.R. *to wall.*)

41

FDR. You're quiet and restful.

ELEANOR. I'm just tired. Is Louie in his room?

FDR. Said he was going out for a feel of the pulse of the city. What he really means, he's going to buy newspapers. Loves the Teapot Dome stories. Adores political scandals—if they embarrass Republicans.

ELEANOR. (*Crosses to* D.R. *door, with chair.*) Franklin, are there other things I should know that you haven't told me?

FDR. You mean like about Louie getting out to get the papers?

ELEANOR (*Crosses* D.R.) I mean about your loneliness.

FDR. Often when you're alone, certain fears seek you out and hunt for a place in your mind. Well, you know I always (*Crosses* D.R.) had a small fear about fire. Since this—that fear sometimes overwhelms me. I've nightmares about being trapped and unable to move. I've been practicing crawling so I can be sure that in case of fire I could get to a window by myself—or to a door or a flight of steps.

ELEANOR. (*Crosses to FDR.*) Yes. I didn't know you'd been— crawling.

FDR. I've been trying and I can do fairly well. But soon I'll be back on my feet. The back muscles came around, and so will the legs. (Crosses L.C. *to boat.*)

ELEANOR. (*Crosses* U.R.C.) Of course they will.

FDR. (*Lifting ship model.*) Like her?

ELEANOR. She's lovely.

FDR. (*Eleanor crosses* L.C.) She'll really sail, you know. She's just not a toy. I miss the sea! (*Places boat on sofa, wheels his chair close to Eleanor and takes her hand as his words come wrenching out of him.*) Eleanor, I must say this, once, to someone. Those first days at Campobello, when this started, I had despair, deep, sick despair. It wasn't the pain; there was much more of that later on when they straightened the tendons in my legs. (*Eleanor sits* U.L.C.) No, not the pain. It was the sense that perhaps I'd never get up again. Like a crab lying on its back. I'd look down at my fingers and exert every thought to get them to move. I'd send down orders to my legs and toes—they didn't obey.

ELEANOR. (*Kneels at FDR's feet.*) Darling—

FDR. I turned to my faith, Babs, for strength to endure. I feel

42

I have to go through this fire for some reason. Eleanor, it's a hard way to learn humility, but I've been learning by crawling. I know what is meant—you must learn to crawl before you can walk. (*Embraces Eleanor.*) (*Door slams offstage* R.)

ANNA. (*Off.*) Mother! Mother! Mother! Mother!

ELEANOR. (*Pulls away from FDR and sits on couch.*) I'm here, Anna. And do be quiet. (*Anna enters* U.R.)

ANNA. How are you, father? Mother I have to talk to you. It's important. (*Crosses* U.R.C.)

ELEANOR. Some other time, dear. I have other important things.

FDR. (*Crosses to* D.R. *door.*) This chamber is yours, ladies. Au revoir.

ELEANOR. (*Crosses* D.R.) Franklin—

FDR. I need the exercise, Eleanor. See you later, Sis. (*He exits* D.R.)

ANNA. (*Crosses* D.R.) Mother, I must talk to you.

ELEANOR. (*Crosses, picks up boat, puts it on shelf.*) Yes, dear, so you told me.

ANNA. I can't talk to you on the run.

ELEANOR. (*Crosses to desk.*) Anna, you can't make up all the rules. I'm listening.

ANNA. (*Crosses to desk.*) It's about my room.

ELEANOR. What about your room?

ANNA. I can not understand why I've been moved upstairs into a little cubby hole, and Mr. Howe has been given my large room.

ELEANOR. (*Crosses* U.R.C.) That change was made weeks ago. Why has it taken you so long to question it?

ANNA. (*Crosses* C.) Because I accepted the change without thinking of it.

ELEANOR. Oh, you did?

ANNA. Yes. But only yesterday, when Granny was here, she asked me the question, direct, and I couldn't give her a clear answer.

ELEANOR. (*Kneels on* D.S. *end of sofa.*) Then, Anna, I suggest you tell Granny to ask me. (*Front door opens off* R.)

ANNA. Mother, it seems to me—

ELEANOR. It seems to me you're behaving badly.

ANNA. I fail to understand—

43

HOWE. (*Off* R.) (*Enters* U.R., *crosses toward* C. *He is carrying a stack of newspapers.*) Ladies. Shall I recount the happenings on the Appian Way?

ANNA. Mother, please—

ELEANOR. Anna, I shall not discuss this with you now.

HOWE. I'm sorry. I'll go.

ANNA. There's no need. Mother and I have concluded our conversation, thank you. Excuse me, please. (*She exits* U.R.)

HOWE. Marie Antoinette couldn't have been more noble on her way to the guillotine.

ELEANOR. It's a busy house, Louie, very busy.

HOWE. A busy world. (*Rattling through newspapers.*) Here's an item I want you to see. The Chicago Tribune. "The New York Democratic Party considers Franklin D. Roosevelt number one choice for Governor."

ELEANOR. Oh, Louie— Those items you manage to squeeze in the newspapers are good reading, but they're pointless.

HOWE. They're good for his morale—and mine. Your morale looks like it's been hit by a Mack truck.

ELEANOR. (*Rises, crosses* U.L. *to* D.S.L. *of desk.*) I have, on occasion felt far cheerier, Louie.

Howe. (U.L.C.) You need a good dinner at Mouquins. I'll take you out tonight, clear your head with a bottle of vin rosé and some snails.

ELEANOR. Perhaps.

HOWE. (*Crosses to Eleanor at desk.*) You're probably scared stiff about that speech you have to read, that's what's wearing you down.

ELEANOR. Louie, I'll be no good at it. I can't lecture. I giggle at the wrong times, can't control my voice, when I shout I think I'm whispering.

HOWE. Eleanor, this work has to be done. You are, for a while, Franklin's eyes, ears and legs. You must go places he can't go.

ELEANOR. I'm certain I'll be awful.

HOWE. You are in the hands of Professor Howe, wizard of the spoken word. Speechless mummies given the eloquence of Demosthenes. Eleanor, you don't have to make anything up, just read it.

ELEANOR. I don't like to read a speech.

HOWE. Do you think the Gettysburg Address was ad lib?

ELEANOR. Louie, I'll try. Leave it at that? (*FDR enters* D.R.)

FDR. (*Crosses* R.C.) Ah, the pulse-taker.

HOWE. (*Crosses* R.C. *to FDR.*) And the pulse is good from Maine to California. The nation still endures under Harding, and Teapot Dome is boiling.

FDR. (*Finger pointed, as though making a speech.*) Scandals or no scandals, this country will be enduring Republican presidents for a long time unless we rip the barnacles off the Democratic organization and make it a modern and progressive political party. I've just finished writing all that to Cordell Hull.

HOWE. (*Crosses* C.) Oh. Eleanor, that's a good theme for your speech.

FDR. My poor retiring Eleanor, being driven into the wilds of the political jungle. Oh, Babs, I invited Marvin and Emmett to dinner tonight. I've got to keep one finger in my lawyer's pie.

ELEANOR. (*Crosses* D.R.) We're not very fancy tonight.

FDR. My law partners aren't very fussy about their food.

ELEANOR. It will be all right.

HOWE. (*Crosses* D.R.) Of course it will. I plan to take your wife to Mouquins for some escargots. (*Eleanor exits* D.R.)

FDR. Eleanor hates rich food. She's too much of a lady to tell you. (*Crosses* U.L.C.)

HOWE. She'll go. Do her good to get out of this place for a while. And now, my friend, we have work to do. (*Crosses* D.L. *to desk.*) I have a list of your various clubs, organizations, federations, fraternities, unions, societies, associations, and groups. You and I are going through this list and do a job of editing. (*Crosses* U.L.C.)

FDR. What exactly have you in mind?

HOWE. The doctors say you're doing too much. I'm merely their obedient servant.

FDR. Let me see that list. You've crossed off almost every organization in which I'm genuinely interested.

HOWE. Franklin, you have too many interests. You've got to cut down. (*Crosses* R. *of couch.*)

FDR. I will not discontinue my work with the Boy Scouts. Their aims are damned important.

45

HOWE. What the hell are you working for, scoutmaster?

FDR. I'll decide what goes and what doesn't.

HOWE. (*Crosses* U.L.C.) All right, Franklin, I'll give you the boy scouts, but something else has to go. (*FDR goes* D.L.C., *Howe follows.*) There's a big breeze blowing, and you have got to trim sails. It's the off year election and you've got to keep your hand in.

FDR. I won't be able to move around too much for a while.

HOWE. But we can write. We can let people know that a man named Franklin D. Roosevelt has opinions, ideas and convictions.

FDR. All right. We can get rid of some of these. (*Missy enters* D.R.)

MISSY. (*Crosses* U.R.) Mr. Brimmer is here.

HOWE. Who's Mr. Brimmer?

FDR. It's a deal I'm working on. (*Warn phone.*)

HOWE. Another? Oh, Franklin.

FDR. (*Crosses to desk.*) Send him in.

HOWE. Missy, who is this Brimmer?

MISSY. The Boss will tell you. (*She exits* U.R.)

HOWE. Is this another one of your imaginative business deals?

FDR. Louie, stop heckling me. Just sit quiet.

HOWE. (*Sits on couch, puts feet on couch.*) Well, I know how you dislike my pacing around. (*Missy, Brimmer enter* U.R. *Missy then goes out* U.R.)

BRIMMER. (*Crosses to* F.D.R.) Good day, Mr. Roosevelt. How are you feeling?

FDR. Coming along, Mr. Brimmer. Mr. Howe. (*Howe waves a greeting.*)

BRIMMER. Mr. Howe, it's a pleasure.

FDR. I've had a long day, Mr. Brimmer. I wonder if—

BRIMMER. (*Crosses back of sofa to table.*) I have the full picture ready for presentation. (*Crosses* U.R.C.) Beginning with the estimates on the construction of the four dirigibles as you requested—

HOWE. Dirigibles?

FDR. Go ahead, Mr. Brimmer.

BRIMMER. (*Mr. Brimmer goes ahead. He is a talker and a walker, and his pacing, it is obvious, gets on FDR's nerves, since he is forced to follow Brimmer's actions.*) The cost of construction, as you will see, will be cheaper if they are built in Germany. Air-

46

ports and masts could be (*Cross* C.) constructed in suitable locations in Chicago and New York for a daily service at comparatively low cost. Also included on this sheet here is the amount of helium gas needed—the cost, the construction, items for storage tanks, etcetera, etcetera. (*Crosses* U.C.) Also listed, approximate cost of personnel to run the ships (*Crosses* D.R.) on a daily basis—the airport crew, ticket agencies, and an advertising allotment based on minimal efforts until the service catches the public fancy. (*Phone rings off* D.R. *Brimmer crosses to desk.*)

FDR. It will catch on.

BRIMMER. I agree, absolutely, I agree. (*Crosses* C.) Charted for you are various (*Crosses* D.R.) hours suggested for best air time in connection with commuter trains, auto traffic and accessibility. Also ideas for campaigns, all to be studied, digested, assimilated (*Crosses to desk.*) and collated. (*Phone in office off* D.R. *has continued to ring since Brimmer started his long speech. This ringing, combined with Brimmer's walking, has made FDR edgy. Howe, who has not moved a muscle till now, gets up to answer the phone, which promptly stops ringing.*)

FDR. Louis, why the hell are you always moving around?

HOWE. I'm nervous. (*He retreats to the corner.*)

FDR. Mr. Brimmer, leave all this here for me. I'll study it in detail and be in touch with you.

BRIMMER. (*Crosses* D.L.C.) We're prepared to seek underwriting—

FDR. We can talk of that later. Thank you, Mr. Brimmer. (*Crosses to desk.*) I'm afraid you'll have to excuse me.

BRIMMER. Of course, I understand. I'll leave these estimates. Mr. Howe, it's been a great pleasure. (*Crosses* D.L.C.)

HOWE. Thank you, sir.

BRIMMER. And good day to you, Mr. Roosevelt.

FDR. Goodbye, Mr. Brimmer. (*Brimmer exits* U.R.) Why the devil didn't someone answer the phone?

HOWE. I don't know. I also don't know about dirigibles. What is this scheme?

FDR. A damned practical one.

HOWE. Between New York and Chicago?

47

FDR. For a starter. We can build this into a transcontinental line, eventually non-stop, coast to coast.

HOWE. Oh, Franklin!

FDR. Don't wet-blanket this, Louie. It could mean a fortune. And I'm sorry I yelled. Brimmer was driving me mad. Prowling up and down like an awkward tiger.

HOWE. (*Crosses* U.L.C.) With a little helium I bet he could get to Chicago. (*FDR laughs, breaking his irritation and bad spell. Eleanor enters* D.R.)

ELEANOR. (*Crosses* U.R.) That must have been a good one.

FDR. Louie's a monster.

HOWE. Madam, your husband is planning to go into the lighter-than-aircraft business, which proves he has a lighter than air head.

FDR. Caution, my friend, is the refuge of cowards.

ELEANOR. (*Crosses* U.L.) Your refuge, Franklin, is bed. You must rest before dinner.

FDR. Very well. (*Crosses* U.R. *to sofa.*) Today I am going upstairs on my own. Out of this room and up the steps on my own. Without helium. (*Pulls himself out of chair and onto couch.*) This is something I've been planning for quite a few days.

ELEANOR. (*Crosses* D.L.) Franklin, perhaps—

FDR. No, now is the time. I can crawl and I'm going to prove it.

HOWE. Some other time, Franklin. It's been a long day.

FDR. I'm going to crawl upstairs to bed. (*Gets on floor.*) Bring the chair along, Louie. Watch me go. (*Sitting on his haunches and using his hands to move his body, he slides backward on the floor and toward the door* U.R. *As he does Eleanor and Howe stand frozen. FDR continues speaking.*) This method of locomotion I shall call the Roosevelt slide, half waltz, half foxtrot. Easy on the feet, and placing all the wear and tear on the derriere. (*He is near the door.*) Well, Eleanor, good?

ELEANOR. Wonderful, Franklin. Wonderful.

FDR. See you later. (*He exits* U.R. *Howe pushes wheel chair out* U.R.) (*Door slams as Eleanor gets to ottoman* C. *and sits.*)

SARA. (*Off* U.R.) Good day, everybody. (*Franklin Jr., and Johnny enter* U.R., *followed by Sara.*) (*Kids cross to Eleanor at ottoman* C.) (*Sara crosses* R.C.)

FRANKLIN JR. Mummy, mummy.

ELEANOR. Hello, boys.

SARA. (*Crosses* C.) I called for them at school. Saved Mademoiselle a trip. And I wanted to try out their French.

ELEANOR. *Les leçons, comment vont-elles?*

JOHNNY. *Très bien.*

FRANKLIN JR. *Absolutment—très bien.*

JOHNNY. Will you read us the end of yesterday's story?

FRANKLIN JR. You promised.

ELEANOR. Wash up and come back. I'll keep my promise. (*Kids run out* U.R.)

SARA. Is Franklin in his study?

ELEANOR. No, mama, he's upstairs. He just went up by himself. Crawling.

SARA. Crawling?

ELEANOR. (*Rises.*) Yes. It's something he's been practicing by himself. He surprised me today by giving me a demonstration.

SARA. But that's too much of a strain. He tries too hard. That's bad for him.

ELEANOR. How can it be bad for him? It makes him independent.

SARA. He can't be seen by the children moving around like that. He can't.

ELEANOR. (*Crosses* U.L., *gets book from shelf.*) You'll have to discuss that with him. I won't. I can't.

SARA. Very well, Eleanor, I will speak to him.

ELEANOR. (*Crosses* C.) Mama, please allow Franklin the freedom of his own mind in this matter.

SARA. He must not be permitted to place such a strain on his body.

ELEANOR. Mama, he's not a child.

SARA. I'll speak to him. Perhaps there is a time when a son will talk only to his mother. (*Johnny, Franklin Jr. enter* U.R.)

JOHNNY. Come on, mummy. Sit down, Granny.

SARA. No, darlings, I can't. I have to see your father. (*Sara exits* U.R. *Eleanor sits on ottoman* C.)

FRANKLIN JR. Mummy, you look tired.

ELEANOR. I am a little, darling. (*Searches for her place in the book.*)

JOHNNY. Mummy, who is older, you or granny?

FRANKLIN JR. Granny is, you dummy.

ELEANOR. (*Begins to read, trying to fight her emotions.*) And today being Wednesday, the merry old shoemaker knew that he could only work on the blue shoes, which were the only ones that were quiet and still on Wednesday. On all the other days the blue shoes would run and play with all the other brightly colored shoes, but on Wednesday they were still and obedient. "Oh, my," said the shoemaker, "what beautiful blue shoes." And he thought to himself that he would make them even more beautiful. So he took his hammer and nails and sat down—and merrily began to hammer away. (*Suddenly, unexpectedly, and uncontrollably, Eleanor begins to cry. She drops the book, turns away from the children and breaks into heartbreaking sobs. The children, stunned, stare at her. Missy enters* D.R., *sees the scene and rushes the children out* U.R. *Eleanor, left alone, continues to cry. After a few moments, Louis Howe appears* U.R. *It is obvious he has been told, because he enters quietly, expecting to see Eleanor. He closes the doors behind him.*)

HOWE. Eleanor, if I can do anything—

ELEANOR (D.L. *Shouting through her tears.*) No, nothing. And, Louie, I hate Mouquins and I hate snails and I'm not going.

HOWE. (*Crosses* U.R.C.) Nobody ever lived who was more entitled to a good cry.

ELEANOR. (*Stops crying, wipes her eyes, blows her nose, straightens her hair.*) I must have terrified the children. (*Crosses, picks up book.*) I won't ever do that again. Not ever. (*Starts to cross out* U.R.)

CURTAIN

PROPERTY PLOT

Act II, Scene 1 to Act II, Scene 2

Strike and Set

Strike:

Paper from Utility Table
Brimmer material from desk L.
Boat materials from Utility Table
  and vicinity
Boat from mantel
Stamp album, Packets, magnifying
  glass from bridge table

Set:

Gold framed Picture from Mantel
  to Bridge Table R.
Ottoman to U.R.C.
Wheel chair R. end of sofa LOCKED
Armchair L.C. to 22 marks
Leg braces (Old) R. end of sofa
  on floor
Crutches R. of Utility Table
6 Letters on colored stationery with
  envelopes, Desk L.
3 Letters with envelopes attached,
  Desk L.
Letter from Montracol Oil Co.—
  Desk L.

Pipe and humidor—Desk L.
Decorative tile on mantel

Offstage R.

Stack of 3 books—ANNA
Illuminated copy of Invictus—MISSY
Briefcase—MISSY
Tray of tea containing: Plate of
  sandwiches, 4 cups, 4 saucers, 4
  cloth napkins, 4 spoons, Pitcher,
  creamer, sugar, saucer of lemon
Slip covers for sofa and armchair
Antimacassar for armchair L.C.
Box of cigars—to be set
Eleanor's notes—to be set
Hat, muffler, heavy coat, gloves,
  rubbers—HOWE
Cigarettes and matches—HOWE
Eyeglasses—FDR
Gloves, hat, muff, coat—SARA

Offstage L.

Babe Ruth Letter—to be set
Bill from golf club—to be set
2 vases of flowers

ACT TWO

Scene 2

We are once again in the New York house living room. A pair of crutches leans against the utility table behind sofa. Near them are FDR's leg braces. Wheel chair is at R. end of sofa. It is January, 1923, Friday. Late afternoon. On the floor at C. are Elliott, Franklin Jr., and FDR. A wrestling match which has been in progress accompanied by yells and groans from the two boys is finally ended when FDR, holding Franklin Jr. with his powerful right hand and Elliott with his equally powerful left, swings them both on their backs and holds them there against their wills.

FDR. Say Uncle.

ELLIOTT. (L. *of FDR.*) Not me.

FDR. (*Applying pressure.*) Just for that, you young lout, you will now have to say Uncle Hiram Joshua Lafcadio Turntable.

ELLIOTT. Ouch. (*Franklin Jr., assuming FDR is occupied with Elliott, has made a move to get away.*)

FDR. Oh, no you don't. (*He applies further pressure on Franklin Jr., without relaxing any on Elliott.*)

FRANKLIN JR. Uncle.

FDR. Uncle who?

FRANKLIN JR. Uncle Hiram Joshua Lafcadio—

FDR. Turntable.

FRANKLIN JR. Turntable. (*FDR frees Franklin Jr., who rises, rubbing his muscles.*)

ELLIOTT. (*Quickly.*) I'm outnumbered. Uncle . . .

FDR. Uncle who?

ELLIOTT. Hiram Joshua Lafcadio Turntable. (*FDR releases Elliott, then sits up on floor.*)

FDR. Next time I shall improvise a few more names for our fictitious uncle. (*Extends his arms.*) Up we go. (*In a manner indicating this is standard procedure, Franklin Jr. whips over the wheelchair, turns it into correct position, then he and Elliott reach*) *out, grab FDR's legs.*) One-two-three— (*They lift, FDR., timing the moves, grabs the chair with his hands, and in a moment, he is sitting in the chair, smiling and confident.*) You two are getting harder to handle. Soon I'll have to draw out my heavy artillery.

ELLIOTT. For a minute we almost had you, Pa.

FDR. Delusions of grandeur. (*Elliott and FDR laugh.*) Boys, today I felt a little more power from my legs—down these heavy frontal muscles, the quadriceps. (*Illustrates on his body.*) The bad spots that we're still working on are in these thick muscles that run down from the hips and buttocks—the gluteus maximus; and then these ham-string muscles on the back of the knees, the gastrocs. Without those I can't balance or get purchase.

FRANKLIN JR. I like the name of those thick muscles.

FDR. The gluteus maximus. Right there.

FRANKLIN JR. That is the gluteus maximus.

FDR. Once I get them all going at the same time you'd better start running. (*Missy enters* D.R., *with the inevitable stack of letters and her notes, together with a framed object.*) Enter Missy, va-moose sons. Your father is a busy man. I'll give you another lesson tomorrow. (*Crosses to desk* L.) (*Franklin Jr. follows as does Missy. Elliott crosses to door* U.R.)

FRANKLIN JR. That's a promise?

FDR. That's a promise.

ELLIOTT. (*To Franklin Jr. as they exit* U.R.) I'll race you up-stairs.

MISSY. (*Crosses to desk. FDR is reading and signing letters. Missy hands him the framed object.*) This came in by messenger.

FDR. (*Examines it.*) A lovely job of printing. I sometimes regret that I told the newspapers one of my favorite poems was Invictus.

MISSY. This is the fourteenth copy you have received.

FDR. By all odds it is the most beautiful. I'd like it hung in my bedroom. (*Hands it to Missy, who crosses to* D.R. *table, puts it down.*) Missy, these letters to the polio victims, they don't sound stuffy, do they?

MISSY. No. They're warm and kind.

FDR. (*Missy crosses* D.L. *to desk, sits.*) McAdoo is so excited over the success of the Democrats in the off-year election he's already counting the votes for himself in 1924.

53

MISSY. He can taste the nomination.

FDR. He's in for a large and bitter disappointment. It's going to be Al Smith. (*He proceeds with the other letters. Howe and Eleanor come in* U.R. *Howe is unwrapping himself from a muffler, hat, heavy coat and gloves. Eleanor is warmly dressed, but not heavily.*)

ELEANOR. (*Off.*) We're home.

FDR. Welcome back.

HOWE. (*Crosses to table* D.R.) You wouldn't be so damned cheerful if you had to go out in this weather. How the hell she stands it I don't know. (*Takes off wraps, puts them on* D.R. *table.*)

ELEANOR. (*Crosses to FDR at desk.*) It's lovely and clear outside. (*Howe sits* D.R., *takes off rubbers, leaves them by chair.*)

HOWE. Oh, my God, it's freezing. (*He notices the copy of "Invictus on the table, picks it up.*)

FDR. How did it go, the speech?

HOWE. Invictus. Another rendition of that sticky verse. Franklin, the devotion of your admirers is stifling. (*Puts it back on table, crosses* D.R.)

FDR. Well, how did it go?

HOWE. Your wife has almost rid herself of those ridiculous giggles. She also makes a point now and then with some degree of effectiveness.

FDR. You mean she was good?

HOWE. Adequate.

ELEANOR. Thank you, teacher. (*Howe sits in chair* D.R.)

MISSY. Was it a good turnout, Mrs. R.?

ELEANOR. Excellent. About three hundred women.

HOWE. Five hundred. That's the figure I gave the press.

MISSY. Five hundred—that's a lot of people.

ELEANOR. So is three hundred. (*Crosses* C.) They listened and signed pledges to word. Franklin, I read your statement on the League of Nations to the council and it received genuinely warm applause.

FDR. Good. Between your speeches, Howe's shenanigans and my statements, we're keeping my head above water. (*Eleanor crosses* U.R.)

HOWE. (*Rises, crosses to* D.R. *table.*) Speaking of water—I re-

54

ceived a letter this morning from one of your associates in the late lamented lobster business.

FDR. A jarring intrusion, as usual.

HOWE. He wishes to know if you have been permanently discouraged by the stubborn refusal of the lobster market to raise its prices. (*Crosses* D.L.C. *to desk.*)

FDR. Losing $26,000 in a lobster business is hardly a joking matter.

HOWE. A bit of a pinch, one might say.

FDR. To add further to your merriment, this is a letter from the Montracol Oil Company—(*Hands letter to Howe.*)

HOWE. Oil company, eh?

FDR. Good?

HOWE. (*As he reads letter.*) Oh, that's very good. You now have two thousand shares—of gas.

ELEANOR. What's this one, Franklin?

FDR. This has to do with the investment I made in oil. They didn't strike oil, they found gas. And there's no immediate market in gas.

HOWE. (*Crosses to door,* U.R.) Think how you could have combined this gas discovery with the dirigibles. See you for dinner. (*Exits, coughing and smoking.*)

MISSY. He'll probably keep coughing and smoking until he's ninety, but he worries me.

ELEANOR. (*Crosses* D.C.) If the incense he burns in his room at night gives him some peace from coughing, why don't you let him burn it in here? I wouldn't mind.

FDR. I would. He'd have the entire place smelling like a bawdy house. (*Eleanor crosses to fireplace.*)

ELEANOR. (*Shocked.*) Franklin!

FDR. Mama made remarks about it this morning—not quite as indelicate, but pointed. (*To Missy.*) Let's call it a day, Missy. You're going to the country for the week end?

MISSY. (*Rises, crosses to door* D.R.) That's me. Twenty above zero and I'm off for a holiday.

FDR. Have fun.

ELEANOR. (*Sits* U.L.C.) Goodnight, Missy. I hope it warms up.

MISSY. Thank you. And goodnight, boss, Mrs. R. (*Exits* D.R.)

FDR. Really went well?

ELEANOR. The house is quiet. The children—are they all home?

FDR. Can't tell the players without a score card, madam. (*Counts on his fingers.*) Anna is in her room reading. Johnny is being read to by Mademoiselle. Jimmy ostensibly is still at Groton. Elliott and Franklin have retired to lick their wounds after a wrestling match.

ELEANOR. I can't stop you from doing that, but do be careful. Your legs haven't healed completely from that last fall.

FDR. (*Wheels to sofa.*) They're coming along fine, all four of them. I spent some time on those today. Soon it will be canes. First I want to handle those crutches without braces, or vice versa.

ELEANOR. Of course.

FDR. (*Pulls himself from chair to sofa.*) Of course, you say. Like you mean it.)

ELEANOR. (*Rises.*) I do mean it. It's just that I don't want you to rush and do any damage. You've plenty of time, Franklin. (*Takes wheel chair D.L.*)

FDR. I've learned something about time. Being unable to rush things (*Eleanor crosses to ottoman, sits.*) along has given me patience. Patience, I think, gives a better sense of when to try for the brass ring or when to enjoy the ride without grasping for anything.

ELEANOR. Oh, yes, Franklin.

FDR. Eleanor, when I first took ill, I planned and dreamed about a bright future, half believing, half pretending, like a child on a carrousel imagining himself a general in command of armies. But for weeks now something his been changing inside of me. I don't know when it began, what minute or day or hour, but today I was fully aware that, despite everything, I feel sure footed.

ELEANOR. "A patient man shall bear for a time and afterward joy shall spring up unto him."

FDR. Shall spring up unto us. I sometimes wonder how many of your cousins are still confounded that we married. (*Eleanor rises, crosses to desk D.L.*) Do you think they still consider me a feather-duster?

ELEANOR. Franklin! There are undoubtedly some members of

56

your family who still believe you didn't get much of a bargain. (*Crosses* U.L.C.)

FDR. I imagine they're reconciled to the truth that I did better than you did. (*Eleanor sits* U.L.C. *on ottoman.*) Actually I think mama's only objection to you was that your family said Rusevelt, while we said Roosevelt.

ELEANOR. Could not a Rusevelt by any other name be just as sweet?

FDR. (*Laughing.*) Not to mama. Thinking back, I can hardly blame some of your relatives. I had a lot to learn and I didn't want anyone to know it. So the truth is I was an awfully mean cuss in those early days.

ELEANOR. (*Rises, crosses to FDR on sofa and sits.*) Never mean. Perhaps inexperienced.

FDR. I was snobbish, haughty. I had the Roosevelt name and the Teddy tradition (*Imitates Teddy's broad smile.*), sauced in with ambition. (*Pats her hand.*) I had to learn something about the human heart. (*Smiles at her.*) I've been learning.

ELEANOR. You've always known a great deal about my heart.

FDR. Cousin, wife, dearest—

ELEANOR. (*Holding her hand and looking directly at him.*) Franklin, when I was an awkward adolescent, I felt unloved, unwanted. With you I have always felt needed, wanted. (*Eleanor puts her head on FDR's shoulder.*) And that is a blessing for which—(*The door* U.R. *suddenly opens and Anna enters, carrying some books.*)

ANNA. (*Crosses to sofa.*) Hello, mother. How are you, father?

FDR. (*Sharply.*) Sis, you've been developing an irritating habit of barging into rooms without knocking on doors.

ANNA. I just wanted to put these books back.

FDR. Then do it, Sis. (*Anna is shocked by the harsh greeting and command. She is on the verge of tears. She crosses to chair* U.S.C. *and leans over to book shelf, drops them, and they clatter to the floor.*) That's a stupid, clumsy way to do it. (*Anna breaks into tears and runs out of room* U.R., *crying. Eleanor and FDR exchange a look.*)

ELEANOR. Rather a sharp attack for a mild offense.

FDR. I'll make it up to her later.

ELEANOR. I'd best talk to her before she runs to granny. (*Rises, crosses to chair* U.S.C., *picks up books and puts them on shelves.*)

FDR. Oh, mama is coming to dinner?

ELEANOR. Oh?

FDR. I hope she and Louie don't snap at each other. Last time they went as far as the dessert before sharp words.

ELEANOR. (*Crosses* C.) That's because at the moment mama has one objective, Louie another.

FDR. I intend to talk to mama about it. (*Gets braces, works on them.*)

ELEANOR. Usually your talks with mama last for fifteen minutes, then they become quarrels.

FDR. I'll time it. Make sure it's a talk. (*Howe enters* U.R.)

HOWE. Change of plans. I spoke to Grace. She's been wondering if I've gotten any uglier. Also, Hartley looked at the postman this morning and wondered if that was daddy. So I'm going home for dinner. (*Crosses to* D.R. *table, picks up wraps, puts them on.*) Oh, I think I ought to report, Anna is seated in the upper hallway looking as though she had been axed and maced. (*Crosses* D.L.)

ELEANOR. I'll try to alleviate the pain. Goodnight, Louie. (*She exits* U.R.)

HOWE. Goodnight.

FDR. Can you breathe through all that?

HOWE. You know me. If I'm on my feet I assume I'm breathing.

FDR. Louie, I'm being reflective. (*Howe sits* U.L.C. *chair, puts on rubbers.*)

HOWE. (*Rises, crosses to sofa.*) That's probably because you're heading for another birthday.

FDR. Having made this one, everything after is velvet. Part of my reflections had to do with you.

HOWE. Ah. I'm fired?

FDR. My good friend, as much as you loathe a sentimental moment, thank you for everything. (*Howe crosses* U.R. *to table, picks up framed poem, crosses* D.R. *of sofa, hesitates, eyes it critically, and looks at FDR, who has been watching him through all this. Howe loosens his muffler, pushes his hat down on his head, takes a mock heroic pose, and then, in a Dutch accent, begins to recite, doing a burlesque rendition.*)

58

HOWE.

> Out of der night that covers me,
> Black as der Pit from pole to pole,
> I tank whatever Gods may be
> For my unconquerable soul.
>
> In der vell clutch of circumstance
> I haf not vinced nor cried aloud.
> Under der bludgeonings of chance
> Mine head is ploody but unbowed.

(*Slowly, during the next two verses, he drops the accent and begins to recite clearly and beautifully—and we see now that what he has been doing is giving a tribute to FDR.*)

> Beyond this place of wrath and tears
> Looms but the Horror of the shade,
> And yet the menace of the years
> Finds, and shall find, me unafraid.
>
> It matters not how strait the gate,
> How charged with punishments the scroll,
> I am the master of my fate:
> I am the captain of my soul.

(*As he has finished, he has spoken slowly, movingly. FDR looks at him. Howe, when he has finished, looks at FDR. There is a pause.*) 'Night. (*Howe walks out* U.R. *FDR throws braces on* R. *end of couch and puts his legs together as if to get up as Anna appears* U. R., *followed by Eleanor. Anna knocks gently at the door. FDR looks up, smiles at her, and then he knocks on the table in answer.*)

ANNA. (*Crossing to him.*) Father.

FDR. Hello, Sis. I'm an old grouch. (*Anna crosses to sofa, sits. Eleanor crosses to braces.*)

ANNA. Father, I've been selfish.

FDR. Now, Sis, no confessionals.

ANNA. Well, I have been. (*FDR directs that she bring his wheel chair to him. She does so.*) I've been mooning around the house

59

like a child. I felt everybody was keeping me out of rooms. I didn't really understand what you've been through. (*FDR pulls himself into wheelchair.*)

ELEANOR. (*Crosses to armchair* U.L.C.) Anna, I've been to blame for some of that. We should have talked before.

ANNA. That's all I ask, mother. Please talk. Everyone is so occupied.

ELEANOR. We'll all try to find more time.

ANNA. (*Turning to FDR. Eleanor sits in armchair.*) And about my room, father. I actually prefer it upstairs. It's quieter.

FDR. (*In wheelchair.*) Anna dear, most of our blessings come in heavy disguises. Which of course reminds me of a story. (*Moves chair toward Anna.*) Way back in the hills of upstate New York, where a lot of poor tenant farmers live, there was a wise old man whom everybody came to with their troubles. One day a woman came to him with a sad, sad story. She and her husband and four children lived in a one-room cabin and she said it was simply unbearable. The old man asked if she had any chickens on the farm, and when she said she had, he advised her to put the chickens into the cabin. She did, and the next day said it was even worse—much worse. Then the old man asked if she owned any cows, and when she said she had two of them, he said "Take the cows into your house." She did and the next day said the place was getting to be a horror. Then the old man asked, "You got a horse?" She said she had. "Take the horse into your house." The woman did that too and the following day said it was just too much, it was awful. Then the old man said, "Well, my dear, I'll tell you what to do. You take the horse and the cows and the chickens and get them all out of there and let me know how things are." And the next day the woman came back relieved and said, "Thank you, oh thank you so much. You can't imagine how comfortable we all are at last."

ANNA. (*FDR embraces Anna.*) Thank you, father, for not putting the chickens in my room.

FDR. Sis, in the last two minutes you've grown ten years wiser. (*One beat.*) (*Door slams off* R.)

SARA. (*Off.*) Good evening, everyone, good evening. (*Eleanor rises.*)

ELEANOR. We're in here.

SARA. (*Off.*) Franklin, too?

FDR. Yes ma'am, present. (*He crosses* L., *Anna crosses* U.L. *Sara enters, loosening coat.*)

SARA. There you are. Anna, you look lovely. (*Anna curtsies. Sara crosses to FDR, kisses him.*) It's bitterly cold. Like a frosty night at sea. Franklin, you look peaked.

FDR. I feel fine.

SARA. (*Eleanor crosses to Anna.*) You're doing too much. I can tell.

FDR. (*Crosses to desk.*) I won't quarrel with you. If you say I look peaked, I look peaked.

ELEANOR. A cup of tea, mama? (*Eleanor exits* U.R.)

SARA. I'd love some. Anna, be a darling. *Tu es très gentille, ma petite.* (*Hands her coat, gloves, hat and muff to Anna.*)

ANNA. Thank you, granny.

SARA. How are all my darlings?

ANNA. The boys are as dreadful as ever. And so am I.

SARA. Were you outdoors today?

ANNA. For a while.

SARA. You have to remember to bundle up warm. Overshoes, gloves, and something soft and woolly around your neck.

ANNA. I know.

SARA. And nurse should be very careful with the young ones in weather like this.

ANNA. (*After a deep breath.*) I heard mother telling nurse that this morning. (*This is possibly the first time Anna has taken this attitude toward granny. There is a brief recognition of this by Sara and FDR. Pause.*)

SARA. Very sensible. (*Eleanor enters with tea tray, crosses* D.R. *table. Sara sits on sofa. Anna exits* U.R. *with Sara's things.*)

ELEANOR. Cream, mama?

SARA. Please. (*Eleanor pours tea. Anna returns* U.R. *and stands by her mother.*)

ELEANOR. Franklin?

FDR. No cream, no lemon, four sugars.

SARA. Cream is good for you.

61

FDR. I don't like cream in my tea. (*Anna hands Sara her tea then hands FDR his.*)

SARA. Thank you, dear.

ANNA. You're welcome, Granny. (*Crosses to Eleanor.*) Mother may I have mine upstairs? I want to finish something I've been reading.

ELEANOR. Of course.

ANNA. (*Crosses to* U.R. *door.*) Excuse me, Granny, Father (*Curtsies and exits.*)

SARA. Anna looks well.

FDR. But I look peaked.

SARA. Franklin, stop being a tease.

ELEANOR. I'm afraid I'll have to be excused. I've got to check on the children. We're all eating together tonight and later we're going to read some Shakespeare. (*Crosses to Sara.*)

SARA. I hope one of the comedies. So much of Shakespeare is too lurid for children.

FDR. (*The crier.*) Tonight—*As You Like It.*

SARA. Lovely.

ELEANOR. Excuse me, please.

SARA. Of course, dear. (*Eleanor crosses to table* D.R. *and exits.*) Oh, Franklin, I'm getting some men at Hyde Park to determine how we can electrify the lift. It is, after all, only a large-sized dumbwaiter and I—

FDR. (*Quickly.*) No. I mean, please don't. The exercise of pulling those ropes is helpful to me. I need it for my arms and shoulders So if you're thinking of me, please don't change the dumbwaiter.

SARA. I feel you're doing too much physically.

FDR. I wish I could do more, Mama. (*Sara rises, crosses to* D.R. *table, puts down cup.*) After all, it's only my legs that are temporarily bothered. The rest of me is as healthy as ever.

SARA. I know that. I know that. I talk to the doctors, they tell me. But sometimes I think that Eleanor—certainly only with motives of deepest love—and that ugly little man, push you too rapidly.

FDR. (*Sara crosses* U.L. *with picture, puts on mantel, takes tile from mantel.*) I don't think so. Dr. Draper doesn't think so. And please, mama, don't refer to Louie Howe any longer with that unpleasant phrase. I've endured it too long as it is.

SARA. (*Crosses* D.R. *to table with tile, puts it on table.*) Franklin, your tone of voice is very disturbing to me.

FDR. Mama, if possible I should like to have a quiet talk with you. I'd like not to quarrel. Now, mama, I know how upset you've been. This is a real wrench for you. But I'm going to get over this. And if (*Sara goes* D.L. *to armchair.*) I don't—a big if—I'll have to become accustomed to braces and canes and wheelchairs. And so will you.

SARA. (*Sits in armchair.*) Franklin.

FDR. Please, let me finish. Louis Howe said (*Sara makes an involuntary grimace.*)—Mama, stop that. Louis Howe told me when I was in the hospital after Campobello that I had one of two choices. I could lie on my back, be a country squire and write books. Or I could get up and become president of the United States. Now I believe Louie's dreams are far too bright. But I've no intention of retiring to Hyde Park and rusticating.

SARA. Franklin, when you were a little boy, your dear father took you for a visit to the White House to see President Cleveland.

FDR. I know, mama.

SARA. (*Rises.*) Let me finish. And President Cleveland said, "I make a strange wish for you. It is that you may never be President of the United States."

FDR. Well, he was playing the odds in wishing that.)

SARA. (*Rises, crosses* U.L.) Your cousin Teddy died because of ambitious people around him pushing him into things. Died because he didn't know when to stop. Didn't know that you can't make it the same world for all people.

FDR. Maybe we can't. But it seems to me that every human has an obligation in his own way to make some little stab at trying.

SARA. It's not such a bad world, Franklin, not at all.

FDR. (*Crosses to* D.R. *table.*) I don't have any personal complaints. I'm lucky. I had rich parents.

SARA. Don't be self conscious about that, Franklin. Advantages of birth should be worn like clothes, with grace and comfort. (*Crosses to sofa for purse, crosses* D.L.C.)

FDR. Yes, yes. *Noblesse oblige,* the poor will always be with us. We went through that when I sold the mining stock.

SARA. On reflection, you must admit that was a childish gesture. (*Sits in armchair.*)

FDR. (*Crosses to Sara.*) I would not hang on to stock bringing me an income over the tortured bodies of miners who lived as if they were in the middle ages. These are different times. The attitude of *noblesse oblige* is archaic.

SARA. (*Rises.*) Franklin!

FDR. It's another name for indifference.

SARA. How dare you!! You're talking to your mother. (*Crosses* D.R.) Even if I were to agree with your romantic political ideas, it's absurd for you to consider running for public office. The traveling and the speeches would be an enormous strain for you; impossible. (*Sits in chair* D.R.)

FDR. At the moment I'm not running for anything, and I won't until I can get around and stand up on my two feet. But that doesn't mean I have to go into hiding.

SARA. I'm not asking you to do that. I'm asking you to be sensible. To take up a permanent residence in Hyde Park, where you could be comfortable, where you could use the time for resting and regaining your strength.

FDR. I love Hyde Park. But I want to use it, not let it bury me.

SARA. That's a terrible thing to say.

FDR. You know what I mean.

SARA. No, Franklin, I don't know what you mean. I only know that your stubbornness is not only your strength but your weakness, and you needn't think for a—

FDR. I needn't do a damn thing. But I'm not going to let myself go down a drain. A bad beating either breaks the stick or the student. Well, I'm not broken. I'm not settling for the life of an ailing invalid. And I will no longer abide implication, innuendos or insinuations that I do so. (*Crosses* D.R.)

SARA. Franklin, I don't want you getting angry. It's not good for you—

FDR. (*Crosses* C., *stops.*) It's damn good for me.

SARA. (*FDR crosses* D.L.) I wonder if you truly know what is good for you. You come by your Dutch stubbornness by birth.

64

And some of that Dutch stubbornness is mine, from long association. (*Rises, crosses* C.) Franklin, many years ago, when I was a little girl, I sailed to China with my father on Clipper ships. On one of those trips, many years ago, as we rounded Cape Horn we headed into a fearful storm. My father, eager and headstrong, urged the Captain to head into the sea, to fight through the storm. But fortunately the Captain of the ship was a better sailor than my father. He wanted to save his ship. He gave orders to trim sails and heave to! We rode out the storm safely, and when the heavy weather was gone, we were able to sail ahead and nothing was lost, nothing. Be wise, Franklin. Ride out the storm. (*FDR crosses* C. *Sara stops him.*) Son, what do you believe I want for you? Obscurity, invalidism? Do you believe that this is my ambition for you? Having been a mother for over forty years, do you think this is what I want? Any dream you ever had or could have, I have. All pain you have felt I have felt. I don't want to see you hurt.

FDR. (*Turns chair, crosses* D.L.) That's enough. There'll be no more talking. No more. (*Sara goes to the side of the room. She is moved and hurt, but genuinely trying to cover her emotions. FDR is trying to cover what he feels. At this moment, Eleanor enters* U.R. *She sees at a glance that there is tension in the room. Sara turns her back a moment, then faces Eleanor, contained but cold. Eleanor crosses to* D.R. *table.*)

SARA. Eleanor, I cannot have dinner with you tonight.

ELEANOR. Mama—you may have quarreled with Franklin—but not with the rest of the family. (*Sara is silent.*) Please?

SARA. (*Reluctantly.*) Very well—I'll join you. Excuse me now, for a little—(*Eleanor nods. Sara looks at FDR. He, by now, is depressed rather than angry. Sara leaves* U.R. *Eleanor watches FDR, who sits glumly in his chair for a moment, then whirls around to her.*)

ELEANOR. Franklin, anything needed? (*She crosses* D.R.C.)

FDR. Nothing. (*Eleanor hesitates a moment, then exits* U.R. *FDR sits for a moment. He is low and dispirited. Suddenly, he looks up and toward the crutches. He is in his mind challenging his mother and what she has implied. He decides to prove something to himself and to her. He quickly rolls his chair to his crutches.*

He places them on his knees, takes off his glasses, puts them o
table, rolls chair to clear section of room, sets brakes on wheel
chair, puts up one crutch and then another, attempting to rise of
the chair by himself and onto the crutches. He is confident and
determined. He is half out of the chair when the crutch slips away
from him and he crumples to the floor. He lies there a moment
a look of sickening defeat and humiliation and pain on his face
He rubs his legs. Then, alarmed that he has been heard, he at
tempts to get back into his chair. This is not an easy task, bu
slowly, carefully, and painfully, he manages—again almost meet
ing disaster, but finally overcoming his obstacles, he makes the
chair. He pauses, exhausted and in pain. Then he reaches for hi
crutches, rolls the chair to each crutch successively, and finally by
stretching and bending, gets them into his hands and over his
knees. Slowly he leans back, then stubbornly, he places the crutche
before him and prepares to try again to rise from the chair. As
he struggles,

THE CURTAIN FALLS

PROPERTY PLOT

ACT III, SCENE 1

Strike and Set

Strike:

Tea set from table R.
Tea cup and saucer from desk L.
Ottoman
Leg braces (Old)
Crutches
Books from table U.L.
Bridge table

Set:

Straight back chair from U.L. to U.R.
Slip covers on sofa and chair D.R.
Antimacassar on armchair L.C.
Flowers (Forsythia) in vase on Utility Table
Flowers (Forsythia and tulips) in vase on bookcase U.L.C.
Crutches Wagon R. against U.R. wall
New braces wagon R. against U.R. wall
Old braces on desk wagon L.

Gold frame picture on Utility Table
Cigarette box on Desk L., D.S. end
Box of cigars R. side of Utility Table
Eleanor's notes R. side of Utility Table
Tweezers on desk L.
Wheel chair on Wagon L.
Ashtray on desk wagon L.
FDR's nomination speech in wheel chair wagon L.
Eleanor's knitting chair L. (Personal)
Missy's briefcase Desk L. (Personal)
Watch—LASSITER (Personal)
Watch, notebook and pencil—MISSY
Eyeglasses, list, vest-pocket watch —SMITH

Off R. Table

2 Scotch and sodas with real ice and 1 tall soft drink on tray—MISSY

67

ACT THREE

Scene 1

It is May 1924. We are again in the New York house. Spring flowers are in vases. It is a sunny spring day.

In the room is Mr. Lassiter. He is a middle-aged man. He is well-dressed and carries an air of authority. He looks at his watch, steals a look at U.R. *door.*

The door U.R. *opens and FDR enters, wheeling his chair, followed by Howe.*

FDR. How do you do, Mr. Lassiter?

LASSITER. Mr. Roosevelt.

FDR. (*Crosses to desk.*) I regret I had to keep you waiting, Mr. Howe.

LASSITER. How do you do, sir. Mr. Roosevelt, I know that your time is terribly occupied, but what I have to talk to you about is of great importance.

FDR. I recognized the note of urgency in your telegrams. (*Howe takes his familiar perch on sofa.*)

LASSITER. (*Sits in armchair,* U.C., *looks at Howe.*) You of course know something of the organization I represent.

FDR. I do indeed.

LASSITER. We have in recent months enlarged the scope of our work and we hope very shortly to have a national pattern of activity. Your name, Mr. Roosevelt, has stood for something important among the rank and file of our membership.

FDR. Please thank the rank and file.

LASSITER. I will come directly to the point. Your chairmanship of Governor Smith's campaign for the presidential nomination has caused much apprehension among many—many of our members.

FDR. That's curious, Mr. Lassiter. What causes this apprehension?

LASSITER. Because of our opposition to Governor Smith we view with alarm your association with and sponsorship of his cause.

68

FDR. I, for one, am very flattered by my association with Governor Smith. What is there about him that induces this opposition from your membership, Mr. Lassiter?

LASSITER. (*Rises, crosses* D.R.C.) Mr. Roosevelt, I don't think it necessary for me to dot the i's and cross the t's.

FDR. I love to dot the i's and cross the t's.

LASSITER. (*Crosses to armchair.*) Well, sir, you must be aware of the fears that many Americans have when they contemplate the election of a Catholic to the presidency of the United States. The domination of the church over its members is well known. And Governor Smith is a devout Catholic. (*Sits in armchair.*)

HOWE. Would he be more acceptable if he were a renegade Catholic?

FDR. Louie! It occurs to me, Mr. Lassiter, that your members might be satisfied with a personal statement from me that would enlighten them on my views in this matter.

LASSITER. (*Rises, crosses to desk.*) I am certain that a statement of the proper kind from you, Mr. Roosevelt, would be of some service.

FDR. (*Crosses* D.R.) I have something in mind. Missy! (*Missy enters* D.R. *carrying notebook and pencil.*) Would you be good enough to type up a statement. How many copies would you like, sir?

LASSITER. (*Missy sits* D.R.) Oh, one or two would be sufficient. We would print it and circulate it for the best effect.

FDR. And I will see that it gets proper circulation in other quarters. (*Lassiter crosses* U.L., *crosses* D.L. *FDR wheels chair so he faces Missy directly. Dictates.*) I am not worried that the Roosevelt name will be tarnished by any association with Governor Smith. If a Catholic who has the ability, broadness of view and the record that entitle him to be considered presidential timber cannot be nominated or elected president because of his religion, then we might just as well be consistent and say he can not be governor or congressman or mayor, or hold any other public office, or be called upon to serve in the army or navy in defense of his country in war. (*Twists chair around, looks at Lassiter.*) Is that what you had in mind, Mr. Lassiter?

LASSITER. Good day, Mr. Roosevelt. (*Stalks out of room* U.R.)

FDR. (*Crosses* U.R. *to door.*) Good day, Mr. Lassiter.

HOWE. (*Missy rises.*) I wonder if there is any way of getting th
tone of voice you used in print.

MISSY. (*Takes chair* U.R., *sits next to FDR.*) Unfortunately ther
are a lot of people who feel exactly like Mr. Lassiter.

FDR. The real issue remains. Is Governor Smith best equipped t
be the nominee for the Democratic party and ultimately presiden
of the United States? I think he is. (*Crosses to desk.*)

HOWE. (*Rises.*) In this year of our Lord 1924, even if Al Smit
were a Protestant and dry he couldn't be elected President on th
Democratic ticket. If he is the right man, he's running at th
wrong time.

MISSY. (*Looks at her watch.*) Right or wrong, the Governor i
twenty minutes late.

HOWE. The convention isn't until June. We can wait. (*Crosse
U.L. to armchair.*)

FDR. (*Looks through papers on desk.*) Missy, would you send
note to the Golf Club along with a check for my dues. "I shoul
like my membership changed from active to non-resident.
(*Pause.*) "I can't possibly play golf myself for a year or two.
The usual thank you ever and very truly.

MISSY. Yes, sir.

FDR. (*Looking quickly at other papers.*) I haven't anything els
Missy. Type up that statement as soon as you can.

MISSY. (*Crosses* D.C.) Have anything, Louie?

HOWE. (*Crosses* D.R.C.) Nothing for paper. (*Missy exits* D.R.
Just a pocketfull of second thoughts.

FDR. Second thoughts? Louie, what's worrying you?

HOWE. First, breathing. (*Wheezes air into his lungs.*) I've bee
wondering what Al Smith wants to talk to you about this afte
noon. (*Crosses* D.L. *to desk.*)

FDR. I would suppose its some genial campaign chatter.

HOWE. I think it's something special.

FDR. What do your psychic rumblings indicate?

HOWE. I haven't yet spelled out all the words on my invisib
ouija board.

FDR. Do you think he regrets his appointment of me as chairman

HOWE. He still needs upstate New York. You're Protestant, dry

70

ural. You're the logical cowcatcher. I've been thinking about Burke Cochran.

FDR. Why Burke Cochran?

HOWE. (*Leans on desk.*) Franklin, ever since Burke died, Smith has been searching for a replacement. He's been trying out speakers to place him in nomination.

FDR. If he's finally gotten around to me it must be a reluctant choice.

HOWE. Why so?

FDR. Oh, Louie, you know that Al has a patronizing attitude towards me. (*Imitating Smith.*) Look, kid, let me teach you the facts of life in the big city.

HOWE. (*FDR crosses* c.) You're one breed of animal and he's another. He made it without a rich family and he's as good as you any day.

FDR. It would be odd for a chairman also to nominate. A precedent.

HOWE. Would you be up to it?

FDR. Sometimes I wonder if I can stand the gaff of active work. Maybe the aspirations and dreams for public service will disappear in the hard light of practical politics.

HOWE. (*Crosses* c. *to FDR.*) I'm no idle dreamer, Franklin. Working with you is an act of faith. I believe God has an eye on your future.

FDR. God has an infinite variety of tasks and I don't believe he's available as a campaign manager. (*Crosses* R. *of sofa.*)

HOWE. (*Follows FDR.*) Franklin the problem is this: to stop a lot of talk from people who say Roosevelt's a nice fellow who once had a fine chance but isn't it too bad. You might be able to carry it off wonderfully and put the party on notice that you're ready for active service. But you could fail and be headed for the political boneyard.

FDR. That's a clean picture of the situation.

HOWE. Well?

FDR. Let's see if Al starts sizing me up as his nominator.

HOWE. And if he does?

FDR. Then Louie *mein* boy, I'll start sizing him up as my nominee. (*Eleanor enters* U.R., *crosses* D.R.C.) Who's going with you, Eleanor?

ELEANOR. (*FDR crosses to desk.*) I don't need an entourage. I walk in, say my few words, shake a hundred hands, and go on to the next stop.

HOWE. Why don't you get Eleanor's opinion on what we've been talking about?

FDR. Louie has a hunch, and I'm inclined to think he's right, that Al Smith is coming here today to ask me to place him in nomination.

ELEANOR. Well, I have heard that he's been shopping around for a speaker.

HOWE. She hears everything.

FDR. Well, what do you think?

ELEANOR. (*Crosses to* D.L.C. *armchair.*) I think it's a decision that only you can make.

FDR. That's taking a well-defined position.

ELEANOR. I know you make a wonderful speech. Whether you're ready to do it is a matter that only you can decide.

HOWE. What about the risks or advantages politically?

ELEANOR. I'm no politician. I have the naive point of view that in public service one should pursue principles without calculating consequences.

HOWE. She's right. She's no politician.

ELEANOR. (*Crosses* D.L. *to* FDR.) Only one point to consider, physically. You'll have to stand for almost three-quarters of an hour.

FDR. Yes. I would have to go into training for that. Mm! I like that cologne. (*Missy enters* D.R.)

MISSY. They're ready, Mr. Roosevelt. (*Eleanor crosses* D.R. *to* Missy.)

FDR. Oh, Eleanor, I wish you'd take a copy of that along with you. If you find a place to use it this afternoon, rattle it in.

HOWE. Hail and farewell.

ELEANOR. Bye-bye. (*Exits* U.R.)

FDR. Good luck. I think Eleanor is beginning to enjoy this political prowling.

HOWE. What's more, she's getting damn good at it. (*Doorbell ings off* R.) (*Missy crosses* L. *Howe goes* D.R.C.) It's late enough. That could be the governor. (*Missy exit* U.R.)

ELEANOR. (*Off* R.) Good afternoon, Governor Smith.

SMITH. (*Off.*) (*FDR crosses* C.) Hello, Eleanor. And hello, Missy.

MISSY. Good afternoon, governor.

SMITH. Why, I've never been greeted by a brace of such beautiful girls. Eleanor, I hear you're getting to be quite a speaker. Glad you're on my side.

ELEANOR. (*Off.*) The fact that I am makes my speeches sound better.

SMITH. (*Off.*) Hope to see you soon. Bye.

MISSY. (*Off.*) Mr. Roosevelt's in the library, Governor. (*Smith, Missy enter* U.R.)

SMITH. Hello, Frank. (*Crosses to FDR.*)

FDR. (*Crosses to Smith.*) Hello, Al.

SMITH. How're you feeling? Hello, Louie.

HOWE. Hello, Governor. You're looking fit.

SMITH. (*Shakes hands with FDR.*) That hand of yours is getting like a vise.

MISSY. Some cold refreshment?

SMITH. (*Crosses* L. *to chair.*) Why Missy, there's a law in this country against strong refreshment. An obnoxious law, but nevertheless a law. (*Crosses to armchair.*)

MISSY. I know. Scotch or rye?

SMITH. Scotch, thanks, and don't kill it with soda. (*Missy exits* D.R. *Smith sits in armchair.*) Frank, I met Eleanor on the way in. She's doing a fine job.

FDR. (*Crosses* D.L. *to desk.*) She's been taking lessons from Professor Howe.

SMITH. Louie, you ought to open up a school.

HOWE. (*Crosses to Smith with cigars.*) Governor, any school in practical politics would have to have you as Dean.

SMITH. Say, I didn't know you could hand out the blarney. Frank, I hear you've broken up your law firm with Emmett and Marvin. What's the matter, was the work a little too rugged for you? (*Howe crosses* C. *by sofa.*)

FDR. (*Howe sits on sofa.*) Matter of fact, Al, it wasn't rugged enough, I did withdraw on the friendliest basis, but their type of

73

business, estates, wills, etcetera, frankly bored me to death. (*Miss*
enters D.R. *with drinks.*)

SMITH. Certainly keeps you freer to do what you want.

MISSY. (*Crosses to Smith.*) There's your scotch, Governor. Stil
alive, I hope. (*Crosses to FDR.*) And yours, Mr. R.

FDR. Missy.

MISSY. (*Crosses to Howe.*) And I brought you a soft drink, Louie

SMITH. Perfect, Missy. Thanks.

HOWE. Reluctantly, thanks.

MISSY. (*Crosses to door* R.) If you need fresh ones, a call wil
bring you our instant courteous service. (*Missy exits* D.R.)

SMITH. That girl's a jewel, Frank.

FDR. That she is.

SMITH. They tell me there's a lot of McAdoo money around town

HOWE. I wish I had some money to bet. Bill isn't going to make
it.

SMITH. He's coming into town a lot stronger than I thought
I'll tell you something, Frank, we're putting on a big show here in
New York, and we can make it look like Smith all through the
city. But McAdoo and his organization are coming to this convention with a half-Nelson on all the rules and program ma-
chinery. We can get strangled inside Madison Square Garden.

FDR. We won't get strangled. Though it's going to be a mighty
tough wrestling match.

SMITH. (*Puts drink down.*) I'd like to win this nomination, but
there's a good chance it could be a stalemate. Some dark horse
may come riding home. (*Puts glasses on.*) I was going over the
delegate strength with Belle Moskovits (*takes list out*) and Joe
Proskauer yesterday. How do you size it up, Frank?

FDR. I don't think you can do it on the first ballot, Al.

SMITH. That's the way we figured it. (*Puts list back in pocket.*)

FDR. But neither can McAdoo.

SMITH. I'll tell you one thing, Frank. If it isn't going to be me,
it'll never be McAdoo. I'll fight him with my last breath. Any man
who can take the support of an organization like the Ku Klux
Klan—he's not my kind of man.

FDR. (*Crosses to desk.*) Oh, a letter reached me and I want you
to hear part of it.

74

SMITH. You handle that chair like a scooter.

FDR. Practice makes "poifect," Al. It's from Babe Ruth. I asked him to chairman a committee for you.

SMITH. The Babe.

FDR. (Picking up letter.) "No, poor boy can go any too high in this world to suit me. You know, we ballplayers travel the country a good deal and I hear lots of fellows talking about Al Smith and his chances to be president, and I'm telling you that most everybody I talk to is with him."

SMITH. How many ball players are there?

FDR. I hope he's as good a prophet as he is a slugger.

SMITH. (Howe rises, crosses D.R.C.) I sure miss Burke Cochran during these days. He had a great instinct in these subtle matters of conventions, nominations and elections. Sort of spooky. I sure miss him. For many reasons.

FDR. You certainly would have wanted him to nominate you. There was no one better.

SMITH. That's a fact. No one better.

FDR. He had a magnificent voice and knew how to use it.

SMITH. It wasn't just the way he talked. He had a knack of saying just the right thing.

FDR. That he did.

SMITH. For days I've been trying to think what Burke would have wanted to say in a nominating speech. (Howe drinks.)

FDR. It seems to me that he'd have argued for you as a progressive. He certainly would have been aware of the issues—The Volstead Act, the Klan, and the latent issue of your faith. But he might have been willing to point out that the obligation above any one candidate is to keep the party together.

SMITH. I'm all for party unity, but I don't intend to temporize on the issue of the Klan. And Burke wouldn't have, either.

FDR. I agree that it ought to be burned out once and for all. But if we can't get through a resolution condemning the Klan, we still mustn't break up the party.

SMITH. Frank, I remember all my early lessons. One of them was that the first objective of a politician is to be elected. Then he can fight for causes. But in the case of the Klan I'm willing to forget an early lesson.

75

FDR. (*Crosses* C. *to sofa.*) There's another issue, Al, that's mor
important than the Klan. The issue of world politics and America'
place in it. Burke would have talked of that, perhaps.

SMITH. Frank, if you're talking about the League of Nation:
that's a dead dodo.

FDR. I believe if the Democratic party is going to stand, it has t
stand for something big and noble.

SMITH. I suppose there's nothing wrong with mankind having
vision of a world organization. But it's only a vision.

FDR. Newton Baker wants to submit a resolution to support th
League of Nations in the convention.

SMITH. It hasn't got a chance.

FDR. Perhaps not, but I think you ought to support it. Woodrov
Wilson's in his grave only three months and I don't think we ough
to let his conviction about the League be buried with him.

SMITH. It's all right with me.

HOWE. I'll talk to the program committee and get Baker on th
schedule.

SMITH. Fine. Frank, got any other notions about what Burk
Cochran would have to say?

FDR. Finally I believe he'd make up his own speech, a large par
of which would have to do with the fine record of the man he'
be nominating.

SMITH. (*FDR crosses* D.L.) Yes, I suppose a few kind word.
about me would be in order. Frank, Burke had a theory that n
nominating speech ought to run more than thirty or forty minutes

FDR. You can read the Constitution in that time.

SMITH. It's a long time for any man to be on his feet.

FDR. A man certainly can't make an effective speech sitting down

SMITH. You can be sure of that.

FDR. After all the months I've spent in this chair, I've come t
love the time I spend each day standing on my crutches.

SMITH. M—hm.

HOWE. Fresh one, Governor?

SMITH. No thanks. Frank, I'd like you to put me in nomination.
(*Rises, crosses* C.)

FDR. That's a surprise.

HOWE. Caught me flat-footed.

76

SMITH. Will you do it, Frank?

FDR. Certainly.

SMITH. (*Crosses to FDR.*) Fine! I'll want to have a look at what you're going to say, and Joe Proskauer may have an idea or two. He's a good phrase-maker.

FDR. (*Smith crosses* C.) I won't mind the addition of a few phrases. But, Al, what I say will have to be what I want to say.

SMITH. Yes, Frank. You have made that quite clear. (*Looks at watch.*) Say, time runs fast. I've got some other people I've kept waiting. (*Rises. FDR crosses* C. *Howe crosses* U.R.) I'm glad you're going to do this, Frank. I appreciate it and I won't forget it.

FDR. (*Howe crosses* D.R.) Thank you, Al. I consider it a singular privilege and honor. And I'll try to make your choice a good one.

SMITH. I'm satisfied you will. Take care, kid.

FDR. So long, Al.

SMITH. (*Crosses to Howe.*) See you, Louie. Say goodbye to Missy.

HOWE. I'll take you to the door.

SMITH. (*With Howe at door, turns back.*) Frank, did you have an idea I was going to ask you?

FDR. A vagrant thought. Why?

SMITH. It occurred to me you were both too surprised to be surprised. (*Smith exits* U.R.)

FDR. Missy! Missy! (*Missy enters* D.R. *FDR crosses* D.R.) I'm going to nominate Al Smith!

MISSY. Bravo!

FDR. I like him. He's as sharp as a blade. (*Howe enters* U.R., *crosses to FDR.*) Well, *mein* boy, I feel like an agent that just had an act booked into the Palace. You have the ball, Franklin. Make him do good, Missy.

MISSY. You know me. I write all of Irving Berlin's music and Franklin Roosevelt's speeches.

HOWE. Smith will make the announcement tomorrow. I'll follow up by flooding him with congratulations.

FDR. Louie, ease up. Missy, we have to get a blueprint of that platform at the Garden. I want to know just how far it is from where I'll be sitting to that lectern.

HOWE. About ten steps, I'd say, not more.

77

FDR. Ten steps. I can do that. I'll take Jimmy with me. He's the biggest. Ten steps—about twenty feet? (*Slow cross to* C.)

HOWE. About.

FDR. I'll work on that. We've got to get the exact measurements. (*Continues crossing* D.L.)

HOWE. (*Follows FDR.*) Work hard, Franklin. They are liable to be the ten biggest steps you ever took in your life.

FDR. Perhaps. Or, to be clinical, I may fall smack on my gluteus maximus.

CURTAIN

Set:

4 wooden stools 38′ platform L.
3 wooden stools 38′ platform R.
Gavel and Block on Lectern
Crutches
Braces in large box
2 copies speech
Screen

ACT THREE
Scene 2

We are in a small room of Madison Square Garden. We ar
aware of the roaring sound of the convention hall which is swarm
ing with delegates. The sound is constant and present in the roor
but not loud enough to distract us.

It is June 26, 1924 at about 11:30 P.M.

In the room is FDR L.C. seated in a more conventional whee
chair than the ones he has used in his home. He is bronzed an
beaming with vitality. James, the eldest son, stands leaning agains
the back wall, holding his father's crutches. Eleanor is seated on
chair across the room L. Howe holds a copy of FDR's speech, th
original of which is in FDR's lap. Missy sits D.R. near FDR.
desk is L. A uniformed policeman is on duty outside. In the roor
is Daly, a fictitious character, who is a bit nervous. The entranc
to the room is in the center of the rear wall. A water cooler i
behind the rear wall, which is made of translucent glass.

A screen is in D.L. corner of the room large enough to cove
FDR and his wheelchair. Next to the wall is a large box whic
holds FDR's braces.

A roar goes up outside. Howe looks at his watch.

HOWE. That very likely is the finish of Miss Kennedy's addres
to the brethren.

ELEANOR. Now what?

HOWE. Now Bill Sweet to second the nomination of McAdoo, the
the roll call, and if Connecticut remembers its cue, it yields to th
Empire State of New York and—

FDR. Then they get one half hour of little ol' me.

DALY. (*Crosses to L. side of FDR's wheelchair.*) Mr. Roosevelt
I've checked everything again and again, and everything shoul
be all right.

FDR. I'm certain it will be, Daly.

DALY. You're feeling okay?

FDR. Fine.

DALY. Is there anything I can do for you?

FDR. No, thank you.

HOWE. Say, Daly.

DALY. (*Turns L. to Howe.*) Yes, sir?

HOWE. I'd like to make sure all is on schedule. Would you go out and check the crowd, get some impressions and then report back. Will you do that?

DALY. Of course. (*Runs out.*)

HOWE. Thanks. Thanks very much.

FDR. Thanks, Louie.

HOWE. (*Missy rises, crosses U.L. to desk.*) I wasn't thinking about you. He was driving me crazy. Franklin, you'd better get ready.

FDR. Jimmy.

JIMMY. I've got them, father. (*Crosses to desk, gets braces, FDR goes behind screen, Jimmy follows with braces.*)

HOWE. Franklin, I'd like to tackle you again about the finish of this speech.

FDR. (*Putting on braces behind screen.*) Louie, not again.

HOWE. Yes, again. This phrase of Proskauer's is a rich one and you're murdering it by not using it at the finish.

FDR. It's close enough to the finish.

HOWE. I think it ought to be the last thing you say. I give you— The Happy Warrior of the Political Battlefield, Al Smith. Period. Crash.

FDR. I don't think so. Period. Crash.

HOWE. You're wrong. It's a sock phrase and it will stick. It ought to be the punch line.

ELEANOR. (*Rises, crosses D.L.*) Franklin, may I say a word?

FDR. Certainly, if you're going to agree with me.

ELEANOR. I've nothing to say.

FDR. That's hardly a sign of wifely devotion. (*Eleanor crosses L. back to chair.*)

HOWE. Your being here and doing this is the most important think. I only feel you're losing the value of the last minute or two of a good speech.

81

FDR. (*Howe crosses to Missy.*) Louie, I'm not sold on changi
it. I'm sorry.

HOWE. Further deponent sayeth not. (*Sara enters.*)

JIM. Did I get it too tight, pop?

FDR. No, Jimmy, that's fine. I think that's fine.

SARA. (*Crosses to FDR.*) Franklin, they hardly let me throug
to you.

FDR. Ah, mama! Ever the lady! You came in just at the rig
time, just as I got into my pants.

SARA. Franklin!

FDR. Welcome to the smokefilled back rooms of politics.

SARA. That howling mob outside is frightening.

FDR. That howling mob consists of ladies and gentlemen co
ducting the business of democracy.

SARA. How anything of consequence can be accomplished out
such a babble is a miracle.

FDR. Mama, I'm all for noisy congregations. God help us if o
conventions ever turn into high school pageants.

SARA. Franklin, this is hardly the time to give me a lesson i
politics. I only wanted a moment to say God bless you. (*Kiss
FDR.*)

FDR. He has given me many blessings.

SARA. And Franklin, speak out loudly and clearly. (*Exits.*)

FDR. Yes, mama.

HOWE. (*Crosses to FDR.*) Franklin, if I know mama, in a coup
of months she'll be writing a political primer. I know this is awfu
but I'm getting nervous.

ELEANOR. (*Howe crosses D.R.*) And I have dropped thr
stitches.

FDR. Sweet's taking a long time for a seconding speech.

HOWE. He's only been on a few minutes. It just seems lon
(*Policeman, Daly enter.*)

DALY. (*As policeman stops him.*) For Godsake, Miss LeHan
will you tell this man I belong here?

MISSY. He does.

DALY. (*Crosses to Howe D.R.*) Sorry, I got panicky. Mr. How
you ought to get ready. (*Crosses to Eleanor D.L.*) The crowd

ormous and busting with excitement. Senator Walsh says it's-
ne to get Mr. Roosevelt to the platform. (*To Howe* U.L.)

OWE. Missy—you check the press handouts. Take Daly for any--
ing you need. (*Daly goes* U.C.)

ISSY. (*Crosses to FDR.*) Right. Boss, I know you'll be tre--
endous.

DR. Thank you, Missy.

ALY. (*Crosses* D.C. *to FDR.*) Good luck, Mr. Roosevelt.

DR. Thank you, Daly.

ALY. (*Crosses* L. *to Eleanor.*) And to you, Mrs. Roosevelt,.
rosses R. *to Jim.*) and to you, Elliott. (*Crosses* U.C. *as to exit.*)

MMY. James. Jimmy.

ALY. (*Leans in to shake hands.*) Oh, yes, of course.

OWE. Okay, Daly, good luck to you. (*Daly exits* L.C.)

DR. Jimmy, are you all set?

MMY. (*Crosses to back of FDR.*) Yes, father. In my mind I've-
ne over it a hundred times. You make the speech and I'll worry
oout everything else.

DR. That's my son, a man of iron. Better check the braces.
Checks braces.) They should be fine. If they slip, pick me up in
hurry. (*Eleanor crosses to FDR.*) (*Jim gets crutches, comes-
ack to FDR.*) (*Howe crosses back of FDR.*)

DR. (*Eleanor crosses to desk.*) I'm ready. Jimmy. Battle stations!
Jim and FDR go U.C.) (*Daly enters.*)

ALY. Mr. Roosevelt— (*Jimmy pushes chair toward exit and*
ns into Daly as)

BLACKOUT

CURTAIN

ACT THREE

SCENE 3

*The scene reveals the platform in Madison Square Garden. W
are looking toward the rear platform. Facing us are huge drap
of bunting and pictures of Wilson and Jefferson.*

*Stage front is the speaker's lectern about twenty feet from th
rear where are grouped FDR in his wheelchair, Jimmy, and thr
or four others including the policeman.*

*At the lectern is a speaker. Next to him is Senator Walsh
Montana, the Chairman. The crowd noise swells loud and turb
lently. It comes from all sides. There is no microphone and th
speakers must yell to be heard. It is bedlam as the speaker tri
to be heard.*

WALSH. Ladies and gentlemen! Please—give the speaker you
attention.

SPEAKER. There is a good deal of mail accumulating for th
delegates in the Convention post office, and we urge you, pleas
to call for your mail. It's getting very crowded. Please call fo
your mail. Thank you.

WALSH. We will continue with the calling of the roll. Connecticu

VOICE. Connecticut, the nutmeg state, yields to the great Empir
State of New York.

WALSH. Ladies and gentlemen. Ladies and gentlemen. The chai
recognizes the Honorable Franklin D. Roosevelt of the State o
New York.

*As he says this there is applause. FDR, whose movements hav
been covered, is revealed standing on his feet, Jimmy to his lef.
He stands for a beat and then, proud, smiling and confident, h
starts to walk on his crutches to the lectern.*

*There is a sudden moment of quiet as FDR begins his walk an
then the applause mounting in intensity. Slowly but strongly an
surely FDR walks those ten great steps. The cheering start.*

histles, screams and rebel yells. FDR reaches the lectern and
nds the crutches to Jimmy who takes them and steps back.
The screaming crowd continues to sound off. FDR stands there
lding the lectern with his left hand. Now he waves his right
nd at the crowd in that familiar gesture. He smiles broadly,
sking in the warmth of this genuine and wholehearted tribute
his appearance, his courage and his future. The cheering con-
nues.

CURTAIN

COSTUME PLOT

FDR

Act I, Scene 1

blue bathing suit, white top, seersucker bathrobe, white linen ha
white sneakers.

Act I, Scene 3

white pair of pajamas, silk scarf, blue bathrobe, black slipper
black socks.

Act II, Scene 1

gray flannel suit, single-breasted, white shirt, blue tie, black shoe

Act II, Scene 2

blue double-breasted suit, striped tie.

Act III, Scene 1

blue blazer, black tie, grey trousers.

Act III, Scenes 2 and 3

blue double-breasted suit, same black tie, and white shirt as befor

ELEANOR ROOSEVELT

Act I, Scene I

white flannel skirt, white sneakers, grey stockings, white slip, whit
blouse.

Act I, Scene 2

l, rust and white striped dress, white apron, red sweater, white
bes.

Act I, Scene 3

ht blue two-piece suit, white blouse, blue shoes.

Act II, Scene 1

een jersey dress, black shoes, white handkerchief.

Act II, Scene 2

ght blue jumper, ecru blouse, brown shoes, brown hat, brown
g, white gloves, furs, blue cape.

Act III, Scene 1

ru dress with pink sash, ecru shoes, straw hat with pink ribbon,
nite beaded bag and white gloves.

Act III, Scenes 2 and 3

hite blouse, two-piece black suit, straw hat with flowers, black
oes, black bag.

LOUIS HOWE

Act I, Scenes 2 and 3

ue pin striped single-breasted suit with vest, Hoover collar
Lindsay arrow), high black shoes, black socks, white shirt with
ench cuffs, bow tie, gold cuff links.

Act II, Scene 1

rown pin striped single breasted suit with vest, brown bow tie
ith dots.

me as previous scene, plus salt and pepper tweed overcoat, grey
omburg, grey gloves, brown scarf, overshoes.

Act III

light grey single breasted glen plaid suit with vest, dark blue b
tie with white polka dots.

SARA ROOSEVELT

Act I, Scene 2

grey skirt, grey taffeta blouse with jabo, grey suede cuban he
shoes with buckle, ecru wool stole, black stockings, pearl earrin

Act I, Scene 3

same as previous scene minus stole plus grey suit jacket, gr
pocket book, grey gloves, feathered hat.

Act II, Scene 1

black taffeta dress, black shoes with buckles flowered hat, go
chain, black braided pocket book, white handkerchief, bla
gloves.

Act II, Scene 2

grey dress with jacket, grey high heel suede shoes with buckl
two strings of pearls, black fur coat, black hat, fur trimmed, bla
fur muff, black pocket book, grey gloves.

Act III

grey lace dress, long jacket, cuban heel shoes, two strings pear
lavendar scarf for head chiffon, beaded pocketbook, grey gloves

AL SMITH

brown chalk striped double breasted suit with vest, white shi
with french cuffs, detachable stiff collar, green and orange, r
rep tie, black oxfords, black socks, gold cuff links, stoma
padding.

MISSY LeHAND

Act I

ue linen dress, white shoes, white purse, white stole, white hat,
ey stockings.

Act II, Scene 1

own crepe dress, brown shoes, amber beads.

Act II. Scene 2

own shirt, beige blouse, brown wool cardigan sweater, brown
oes.

Act III, Scene 1

ey skirt, white silk blouse, navy shoes.

Act III, Scenes 2 and 3

me as previous scene plus grey jacket matching skirt in previous
ene, navy blue silk hat with brim, navy blue purse, white gloves.

ANNA ROOSEVELT

Act I, Scene 1

athing suit, purple, blue skirt with petticoat, white stockings with
arters, black flat shoes, white sailor blouse and hair fall.

Act I, Scene 3

ed plaid skirt, with blue smock, black flats and black stockings,
lue cape.

Act II, Scene 1

laid skirt (same as previous scene), white blouse, long sleeve,
lue pullover sweater, cape, beret.

Act II, Scene 2

rew jumper, white blouse (silk), black shoes and stockings.
ecklace.

89

same as previous scene.

JAMES ROOSEVELT

Act I, Scene 1

black bathing suit, white sneakers, pongee shirt, khaki short
grey short sleeved pullover sweater, brown belt, khaki knee sock
brown shoes.

Act I, Scene 2

grey pajamas, rust colored bathrobe, white sneakers.

Act III

dark blue single breasted suit with vest, white shirt with detac
able collar and french cuffs, black shoes, black socks, maroon ti
gold cuff links, black belt.

ELLIOTT ROOSEVELT

Act I, Scene 1

black bathing suit, white sneakers, brown shoes, long argyle sock
khaki shorts, pongee shirt, brown belt.

Act II, Scene 2

brown corduroy knickers, brown socks, brown shoes, white shir
grey cardigan sweater.

Act III

same as previous scene plus blue tie and tan jacket.

FRANKLIN JR.

Act I, Scene 1

black bathing suit, khaki shorts, khaki blouse, argyle knee socks
brown shoes, brown belt.

Act II, Scene 1

own corduroy knickers, brown socks, brown shoes, tan corduroy cket, white shirt, blue knit tie, tan corduroy hat.

Act II, Scene 2

me as previous scene except tan blouse, no tie, no jacket, no hat.

Act III

me as Act II, Scene 1 but no cap.

JOHN ROOSEVELT

Act I, Scene 1

lack bathing suit, 2 piece, sailor suit, white sneakers, blue ankle cks.

Act I, Scene 3

ame as 2nd change in previous scene.

Act II, Scene 1

rown shorts, brown shoes, brown socks, pongee shirt (tan), rown sweater.

EDWARD

vhite shirt, soft collar, black knit tie, grey jacket (mess), charcoal grey tropical trousers, white socks, white sneakers.

MARIE

vhite petticoat, white stockings, blue oxfords, white skirt, white louse, gold cuff links, black ribbon bow.

MR. LASSITER

blue checkered, single breasted suit with vest, white shirt, detac[h] able collar, blue tie, french cuffs, silver cuff links, black button[ed] shoes, blue socks.

MR. BRIMMER

brown charcoal striped double breasted suit with vest, brow[n] oxfords, brown socks, white shirt with cuffs and stiff collar, gree[n] and black tie, gold cuff links.

DR. BENNETT

3 piece grey herringbone tweed suit, white shirt (marley collar[)] raspberry tie, black high top shoes.

DALY

grey wool single breasted suit with vest, white shirt with detach[?] able collar, and french cuffs, gold cuff links, black shoes, blac[k] socks.

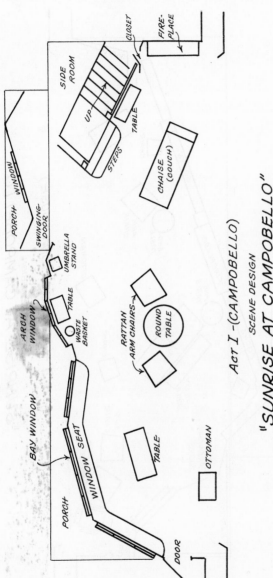

CLOSET

FIRE-
PLACE

SIDE
ROOM

PORCH
WINDOW

UP

SWINGING-
DOOR

STEPS

TABLE

CHAISE
(DOUCH)

UMBRELLA
STAND

ARCH
WINDOW

TABLE

WASTE
BASKET

RATTAN
ARM CHAIRS

ROUND
TABLE

BAY WINDOW

WINDOW SEAT

TABLE

OTTOMAN

PORCH

DOOR

Act I -(CAMPOBELLO)

SCENE DESIGN

"SUNRISE AT CAMPOBELLO"

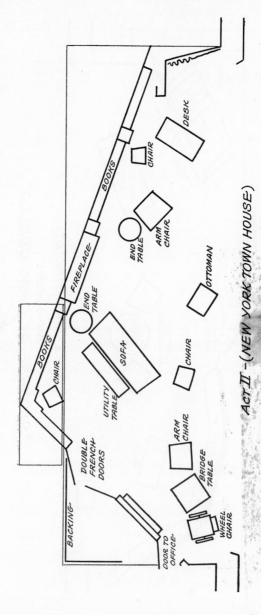

ACT II — (NEW YORK TOWN HOUSE)

SCENE DESIGN

"SUNRISE AT CAMPOBELLO"

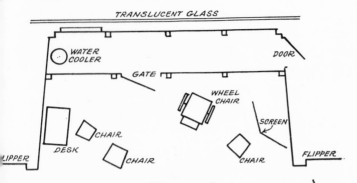

ACT III - SCENE 2

(Ante-Room) MADISON SQUARE GARDEN

ACT III - SCENE 3

(The Platform) MADISON SQUARE GARDEN

SCENE DESIGNS

"SUNRISE AT CAMPOBELLO"

70
71
72
74
75
76
77
79
80
83
85
89